The Unions

THIRD EDITION

structure, development, and management

Marten Estey

The Wharton School,
University of Pennsylvania

HARCOURT BRACE JOVANOVICH, INC.
New York   San Diego   Chicago   San Francisco   Atlanta
London   Sydney   Toronto

Printed in the United States of America
Library of Congress Catalog Card Number: 80-83972
ISBN: 0-15-592952-6

Foreword
to the First Edition

As a long-time student of the labor movement, a diligent and respected researcher, and a teacher with a sense of balance and synthesis, Professor Estey was an obvious candidate to write this book. It is never easy to reduce great quantities of knowledge about a subject—particularly one in which the writer excels—to a lean muscular work that embraces all aspects while also providing some of the fat of detail and insight. Professor Estey has indeed done both. He has reduced a substantial body of material to a clear, concise statement, and somehow—and this is the essence of his art—he has managed to ease its terseness with a style and readability that will attract a wide range of readers in and out of the academic world.

If one could have but one book with which to become conversant with the American labor movement, one would be wise to choose this new study by Marten Estey.

Leonard Sayles
Columbia University

Preface

This book was written primarily for the student—whether in college or in business—who wants a brief but analytical account of what unions are, why they behave as they do, and how they are managed, as well as an account of the rules under which they operate.

The primary emphasis is on the nature of unions as organizations and on the similarities and differences between unions and the business organizations with which the majority of them deal. Accordingly, the text includes analyses of (1) the patterns of union growth; (2) the evolution of union organizational forms and models in response to changing needs and circumstances; (3) the present organizational structure of the American labor movement and the functions of its components; (4) the business-like versus the democratic aspects of union behavior; and (5) the decision-making process within unions.

In recognition of the fact that most of today's college students were born a generation after the problem of labor's civil rights was as burning a public issue as the civil rights of minorities is today, a chapter is devoted to the historic development of the law with respect to unions. Finally, a chapter has been added assessing the impact of collective bargaining, the principal activity of labor organizations.

If this analysis substitutes light for some of the heat which readers of all persuasions are apt to bring to the subject, it will have served its purpose.

Marten Estey

Contents

The Changing Dimensions of the Labor Movement

1

The American labor movement (a collective term for labor unions and employee associations[1] with headquarters in the United States) is a complex institution, the culmination of over 180 years of activity, of expansion and contraction, of ebb and flow. It is the resultant of a myriad of economic and social forces, personal influences, and chance events. Like other social institutions, it is no monolith, but is composed of vastly varied components ranging from the miniscule to the gigantic, from the young to the old, from the declining to the expanding.

Its dynamic character is demonstrated by the fact that the years 1964–1978 witnessed a structural change in the American labor movement comparable in significance if not in scope to the organization of the mass production industries in the 1930's. We refer, of course, to the rapid growth of labor organization among public employees and the rise in their total membership from 1,453,000 in 1964 to 6,019,000 in 1978, a gain of over 4.5 million members.[2]

This significant increase in public employee membership is due to the combined effects of a 150 percent increase in union membership in the public sector and to the fact that during this period an increasing number of professional employee associations (many of whose mem-

[1]Perhaps the basic difference between unions and employee associations is that collective bargaining over the terms of employment is the primary function of unions but not necessarily of employee associations, many of which have assumed that role only recently.

[2]1978 figure from U. S. Department of Labor, Bureau of Labor Statistics, "Labor Union and Employee Association Membership—1978," Press Release, September 3, 1979, p. 3.

Unless otherwise indicated, all 1978 membership data that follows are from this press release, or from unpublished data provided by courtesy of the BLS from its forthcoming *Directory of National Unions and Employee Associations, 1979.*

bers—e.g., teachers—are public employees) and state public employees associations engaged in collective bargaining and were listed as labor organizations for the first time. This phenomenon is so recent that employee association membership was not available before 1968, when it was first reported to be 1.7 million.

Because of the high percentages of women and of white-collar workers among public employees, the rapid growth of organization in the public sector has led to a major breakthrough in the organization of both women and white-collar workers, each of whom now constitute approximately a quarter of the total membership of American labor organizations. Equally important, this growth of organization has meant the emergence of collective bargaining as a major force in the public sector of the economy.

Total Membership

In 1978, contrary to popular belief, union membership in the United States was at an all-time high of 20,238,000.[3] Add to this figure another 2.6 million members of employee associations, and the net result is that membership of labor organizations in the United States totaled 22.8 million in 1978. These 22.8 million employees constituted 22.7 percent of the civilian labor force, and 26.6 percent of all employees in nonagricultural establishments. Because about one-fifth of the employees in private nonagricultural establishments are supervisory and managerial employees not normally eligible for union membership, it is probably fair to say that labor organizations in the United States now include more than one-third of those eligible to join.

Membership Trends

To put these figures into meaningful perspective, let us look briefly at the trends they reflect. Unionism of the size and scale we know today is a fairly recent phenomenon, for although unions appeared in the United States before 1800, total membership in 1900 was still less than 1 million. Not until 1937 did union membership permanently pass the 5 million mark, and only since 1950 has total membership been consistently above the 15 million level. What might properly be called the modern labor movement, in fact, may be said to have started in 1933.

In that year, things looked bleak indeed for the labor movement. Union membership had dropped below 3 million, to the lowest level

[3]Another 1.5 million members of American unions were outside the United States, mostly in Canada, and are not included in this figure.

in seventeen years; only one of every nine employees in nonagricultural establishments, and only one of every twenty people in the labor force as a whole, belonged to a union. So grim was the outlook, in fact, that Professor George E. Barnett, a distinguished labor economist and historian, in his presidential address to the American Economic Association in 1933 prophesied: "I see no reason to believe that American trade unionism will so revolutionize itself within a short period of time as to become in the next decade a more potent social influence than it has been in the past decade."[4]

In fact, however, 1933 proved an historic turning point for organized labor. Starting in that year, total union membership, spurred first by New Deal labor legislation, then by the emergence of the CIO as a competitor to the AFL, and finally by World War II, underwent an expansion unprecedented in both amount and duration, more than quadrupling in the decade 1933–1943 and continuing with only an occasional interruption until 1956, when it reached a peak of 18,477,000, a figure more than six times that of 1933. Meanwhile, the proportion of union members in the United States had risen to include one of every three employees in nonagricultural establishments and one in four of the total labor force.

Immediately following this peak, union membership fell into a five-year decline, so that by 1961 total membership had dropped by more than a million, the most severe and protracted slump in union membership since the doldrums of the 1920's.

The mid-1950's proved, in retrospect, to be another turning point for unions, although of a different kind. What has become a basic problem for the unions is that membership increases have not kept pace with the overall rise in employment, with the consequence that the union's share of the labor market has been declining for the past quarter century. *This* is the proper meaning of the term "the decline of the unions."[5]

Thus in 1978, only 20.2 percent of the civilian labor force belonged to a union, as compared with a peak of 25.3 percent in 1953, during the Korean War. And this represents a 20 percent shrinkage of the market share held by unions—a matter of obvious concern.

But an even more fundamental problem is revealed by another measure of market share—the ratio of union membership to nonagricultural payroll employment. Generally speaking, nonagricultural payroll employment conforms more closely to the market for union membership than does the civilian labor force as a whole. It is a matter of

[4]George E. Barnett, "American Trade Unionism and Social Insurance," *American Economic Review,* Vol. XXIII (March 1933), p. 6.

[5]Much of the material in the next few pages has previously appeared in Marten Estey, "The State of the Unions," *Executive* (Graduate School of Business and Public Administration, Cornell University), Volume 6, Number 2, Spring 1980, pp. 15–17.

crucial concern to the labor movement, then, that union membership in 1978 represented only 23.6 percent of nonagricultural employment, down from 34.7 percent in 1954 (and even more from the World War II peak of 35.5 percent). By this measure, the union's share of the labor market had shrunk almost one-third in twenty-four years.

It is worth noting, however, that the employee associations have been growing at a faster rate than either the labor force or nonagricultural employment. In spite of a slight drop in membership from 1974 to 1978, membership in employee associations rose from 2.3 percent of the civilian labor force in 1968 to 2.6 percent in 1978, and from 2.7 percent to 3.0 percent of nonagricultural employment.

This overall picture is the resultant of two other new and contradictory trends that began in the mid-1950's. One is the long-term decline of organized labor's (in this case, the union's) share of the private sector labor market—the source of the overall decline in market penetration by organized labor. The other is the long-term rise of labor's share (in this case, *both* the union's and employee association's) of the public sector labor market. Here we are witnessing a structural change in the American labor movement comparable in significance to the organization of the mass-production industries in the 1930's. Reported membership in the public sector has risen from 915,000 in 1956 to 6,019,000 in 1978, a gain of over 5 million members. And in state and local government, where membership has grown most rapidly, labor's share of the market has risen from 27 percent in 1968 to 36 percent in 1978.

Relationship of Membership Trends to Labor Force Trends

The seeming paradox of a long-term decline in the ratio of union membership to nonagricultural employment, coinciding with a long-term rise in union membership, reflects the fact that nonfarm employment not only expanded by 65 percent between 1956 and 1978, but has also undergone significant internal changes, involving shifts away from the well-organized industries and occupations to those in which unions had been less successful. Although these challenges have been met with considerable success, as we shall see, it is worth indicating briefly the nature of the changes and the challenges that had to be met.

The most significant changes in the structure and composition of the labor market are quite clear—a continuing shift *from* the goods-producing industries, the traditional stronghold of unionism in the United States, *to* the service-producing industries; and closely related to that, shifts from blue- to white-collar occupations, and from male to female employees. Taken together, these changes in the industrial, occupational, and sex composition of the nonfarm labor force have had a far-reaching impact on the labor movement, and there is every indication that these trends will continue.

Shifts from Goods-Producing to Service Industries

In 1956, when the detailed information on the composition of the labor movement was first reported by the Bureau of Labor Statistics, it was primarily a male, blue-collar movement, with nearly two-thirds of its total membership in the goods-producing industries—48.8 percent in manufacturing, 11.7 percent in construction, and 2.9 percent in mining—and only in transportation, with 15.1 percent of membership, was there substantial strength in the service-producing industries.

But the goods-producing industries did not share fully in the 65 percent expansion of nonfarm employment between 1956 and 1978; employment in goods-producing industries rose only 20 percent, while in the service-producing industries it rose 93 percent. And the industries in which union membership was concentrated in the mid-1950's generally fared even worse; employment rose only 2 percent in mining, 15 percent in transportation and public utilities, and 18 percent in manufacturing. Only the construction industry, where employment rose 38 percent, did better than the goods-producing industries as a whole.[6]

At the same time, employment increases in the service-producing industries (except transportation and public utilities) ranged from nearly 80 percent in wholesale and retail trade to 146 percent in the services, all industries in which unions generally had been relatively weak. The public sector, which has proved to be such a fertile field for union growth, grew 113 percent, mostly due to the 136 percent growth of state and local government employment; the federal sector grew only 25 percent.[7]

Shift to White-Collar Occupations

The shift from the goods-producing to the service-producing industries had a further consequence—it significantly altered the occupational composition of the labor force, from blue-collar to white-collar, a change which may have had more profound consequences for the labor

[6]See the *Monthly Labor Review*, August 1980, p. 69.
[7]*Ibid.*

movement than the industrial shift alone. For in 1956, union membership was not only concentrated in the goods-producing industries, but
an even higher percentage of total union membership—more than 85
percent—was in blue-collar occupations.

It is perhaps symptomatic, then, that union membership suffered
a sharp decline after 1956, when for the first time the number of white-
collar workers (25.6 million) exceeded the number of blue-collar
workers (25.2 million).

The shift to the white-collar occupations has continued, so that by
1978, white-collar employment (47.2 million) was 50 percent greater
than blue-collar employment (31.5 million).[8]

Shift to Employment of Women

Historically, the American labor movement has been essentially a mas-
culine preserve. There have always been important exceptions, of
course—as early as 1920, unions in the clothing industry accounted for
over 40 percent of women in the labor movement—but as recently as
1956, more than 80 percent of all union members were male.

If this pattern had continued basically unchanged, it would have
further compounded the difficulties of the labor movement. But the sex
composition of the labor force, like its industrial and occupational composition, changed substantially between 1956 and 1978. The number of
women in the labor force rose from 21.5 million in 1956 to 41.9 million
in 1978, a gain of over 20 million, or 95 percent. The number of men,
on the other hand, rose only 13.4 million (from 45.1 million to 58.5
million) or 30 percent.[9] As a consequence, the percentage of women in
the labor force rose from 30 percent in 1955 to 41.7 percent in 1978,
in an acceleration of the slow but steady rise in female employment,
which has been evident since 1900.

Behind all these shifts in the composition of the labor force lies
another economic factor—technological change and rising productivity.
Whether we call it automation or not is immaterial; the fact is that until
very recently rising productivity in the production industries made it
possible to produce more goods with the same number of workers, or
even more goods with fewer workers. Accordingly, output has risen
without a corresponding rise in employment or in union membership
in the production industries. Rising output has also increased the need
for labor in the distributive and service industries and thus has aug-

[8]Op. cit., p. 65.
[9]Adapted from the *Economic Report of the President*, 1980, p. 236.

mented the shift of employment from the production to the service industries.

Technological change also has increased the efficiency with which the housewife performs her domestic chores and has released her for outside employment at a time when employment opportunities are expanding in white-collar and service-industry occupations, which may be generally more suited to women's economic needs and training than production or blue-collar jobs.

The substantial shifts of the labor force away from the industrial, occupational, and sex base of the unions of the 1950's may go far in explaining the decline in union membership as a proportion of nonfarm employment. But that decline may be of minor importance compared with the changes in union structure and the composition of its membership dictated by these labor-force shifts.

The Distribution of Membership

The profile of the composition of the labor movement in 1978 provides some measure of the extent to which it has been able to adjust and adapt to the sweeping changes in the composition of the labor force since the mid-1950's.

Industrial Distribution

We have already noted that it is the private sector that has been the source of the overall decline in the share of the labor market represented by union membership. But the problem is distinctly different in the manufacturing and nonmanufacturing sectors of the economy.

In manufacturing, long regarded as the traditional stronghold of organized labor, the most critical current problem is that between 1974 and 1978 the number of union members fell by over 1 million. Union membership in manufacturing reached a peak of 9.2 million in 1968, in the middle of the Vietnam War. And it continued at approximately this level until 1974, when unions still claimed 9.1 million members, down less than 1 percent from the peak.

But between 1974 and 1978, union membership in manufacturing fell from 9,144,000 to 8,119,000, a drop of more than 11 percent. And no econometric model is needed to predict that when the 1980 data become available, union membership in manufacturing will be even lower, as a consequence of the almost daily layoffs and plant closings in the auto and steel industries and of the decline in construction activity to a five-year low.

And here we have the basis for the decline of the union's market share in manufacturing from 51.3 percent in 1956 to 39.9 percent in 1978, a slide of 11.4 percentage points, over half of which has taken place between 1974 and 1978.

In nonmanufacturing, on the other hand, the problem is not lack of membership growth but the fact that employment is growing much more rapidly than membership. Nonmanufacturing membership rose from 8.9 million in 1968 to 10.2 million in 1978, a gain of 1,217,000 or more than 13 percent. But meantime, nonmanufacturing employment rose 37 percent, almost three times as fast as union membership. The result was that organized labor's share of this market fell from 24.6 percent in 1968 to 20.3 percent in 1978.

The bright spot in the picture, as we have indicated, has been the growth of membership in the public sector, especially at the state and local levels. Union membership in state and local government nearly tripled between 1968 and 1978, rising from 764,000 to 2,205,000, and membership in employee associations rose 40 percent, from 1.7 to 2.4 million. The combined share of the state and local labor market rose from 27 percent in 1968 to 36 percent in 1978.

Although unions have not yet caught up with employee associations in terms of total membership among state and local government employees, they are growing more rapidly—clear evidence that after a decade of competition with employee associations, unions have effectively adapted to this new market of professional, white-collar employees. The view that unions cannot appeal to this type of worker is clearly unwarranted.

Labor organization in the federal government has remained virtually stable in the decade 1968–1978, doubtless reflecting the fact, surprising as it may be, that federal employment has risen less than 1 percent during that time.

The approximately 1.4 million union members in the federal government (less than 50,000 federal employees belong to employee associations) represent 50 percent of all federal employees, and one may speculate that this ratio is likely to persist.

White-Collar Membership

Data on the number and distribution of white-collar union members is limited and has been available only since 1956. In that year it was estimated that 2,463,000 white-collar workers belonged to American unions and that they represented approximately 13.6 percent of total membership. During the slump in union membership from 1956 to 1961, white-collar membership fell off more than proportionately, so that by 1960 these workers represented only 12.2 percent of overall membership. Between 1960 and 1978, however, the situation changed dramatically. The number of white-collar workers in unions nearly doubled, to 4.3 million, representing 20 percent of all union members. And when we add the employee associations, whose 2.6 million members are all counted as white-collar workers, we get a total white-collar membership in 1978 of 6,855,000, who together constitute 28 percent of the combined membership of unions and associations.

Much of the rapid growth of white-collar membership, of course, is directly associated with the growth of labor organization in the public sector. Over half the gain is due to the inclusion of the employee associations, 95 percent of whose members are not only white-collar workers but government employees as well. And the growth of the Teachers Union and the State, County, and Municipal Employees added an estimated 750,000 more white-collar government employees during this period.

Women Members

Equally important is the rising proportion of women in the labor movement. In the twenty-four years between 1954 and 1978, the *number* of women belonging to labor organizations more than doubled, from 3.0 to 6.7 million; and the *proportion* of women rose from 17 percent to 27 percent of total membership.

Three-quarters of these women members belong to unions, and one-quarter to employee associations, whose membership in 1978 was 60 percent female.

The female members of unions and employee associations tend to be concentrated in certain industries and organizations. The National Education Association has the largest number of women members—an estimated 910,000—followed by the Teamsters (481,000) and the State, County and Municipal Workers (408,000). Add to these figures the women members of the Retail Clerks (before its merger with the Meat Cutters), the Clothing Workers, the Electrical Workers (IBEW), the Service Employees, and the Teachers, each of which claims over 300,000 female members, and we find that eight organizations account for over half of all women in labor organizations.

On the other hand, one-tenth of all national unions still report no women members, while in another third, women represent less than 10 percent of the membership. All employee associations report women members, and only three have less than 10 percent women members.

Although women now account for more than one of every four members of labor organizations, this is not yet reflected in union or association leadership. In 1976, for example, women accounted for only about 7 percent of all union officers and about 25 percent of the officers of employee associations.

As president of the Coalition of Union Women, Joyce Miller pointed out to the AFL-CIO convention in 1979, "There is an absence of women at the top level of the labor movement."[10] Indeed, there had been *no* women on the AFL-CIO Executive Council, the governing body between conventions. But the situation has now changed: in August 1980, Ms. Miller, who is also a vice-president of the Amalgamated Clothing and Textile Workers, was elected to the Executive Council, the first woman member since the AFL-CIO was founded, and the first member not a president of a national union.[11]

Geographic Distribution of Membership

Although the dynamics of change in the labor force have produced long-run shifts in its industrial and occupational composition, they have not altered the fact that the labor movement in the United States is a predominantly urban phenomenon.

Accordingly, in 1978, New York state had the largest *number* (2,753,000) and the highest *proportion* (39.2 percent) of union members; California had 2.2 million members; and Pennsylvania, Illinois, Ohio, and Michigan had over a million union members each. Together these six states accounted for more than half of U.S. union membership (10.5 million) and nearly half of all association members (1.1 million).

At the other extreme were South Dakota (25,000) and Wyoming (28,000), and four other rural states with less than 50,000 union members each—Vermont, North Dakota, Alaska, and Idaho. These six rural states had a combined membership of only 210,000, or barely 1 percent of U.S. union membership, and barely 3 percent of all association members (65,000).

In relative terms, the least unionized state continued to be North Carolina, whose 147,000 union members represented only 6.5 percent of its nonagricultural employment.

[10]*Proceedings,* AFL-CIO Convention, November 1979, p. 283.
[11]*New York Times,* August 21, 1980, pp. 1, 12.

Long-Run Membership Growth Cycles

Concentration on short-run changes in union membership has tended, in recent years, to produce a situation in which gloomy predictions of stagnation alternate with enthusiastic refutations, depending on year-to-year fluctuations in membership.

A look at the long-run pattern of union growth, however, may provide a more dispassionate standard by which to evaluate the situation. It shows clearly that rapid expansion is the exception rather than the rule. The American labor movement has never grown steadily and evenly; its greatest gains have come in spurts, during which unions have made significant and usually lasting breakthroughs into new territory.

Thus in the forty-five years between 1933 and 1978, union membership in the United States has grown from a low of 2.8 million in 1933 to 20.2 million in 1978, a gain of 17.4 million members. But the bulk of this growth has been concentrated in four short periods of four years each, when membership rose both rapidly and substantially, as shown below:

Years	Net Gain (000's)
1933–1937	2,758
1940–1944	5,098
1949–1953	2,427
1964–1968	2,075

In these four periods of rapid growth, totaling sixteen years, the combined membership gains amounted to 12.3 million, or 70 percent of the total membership gain from 1933 to 1978.

These figures reveal two other significant facts about overall union growth. First, union growth has been closely associated with war; three of the four spurts in union membership in the past half-century occurred during wartime, and one other major growth period took place during World War I.

Second, it seems clear that periods of significant union growth have been identified with a major *external* stimulus—aside from the stimulus of war, the other major expansion of union membership in the past fifty years is linked with the passage of favorable legislation, specifically the Wagner Act. Leadership changes, such as Lane Kirkland's succession to the presidency of the AFL-CIO, have not in the past produced much change in the rate of growth of union membership, although John L. Lewis's founding of the CIO was closely associated with the growth period 1933–1937.

Individual Union Membership Changes

The rise and fall of membership of the labor movement as a whole does not reflect similar rises and falls for each national union; instead, the overall pattern is a composite of divergent trends, the net result of a variety of movements. Even during the sharpest declines in total union membership, some unions will expand and grow; even the most exuberant periods of overall growth are not shared by all unions.

Indeed, since each union operates in an economic and social environment which differs from that of any other union (in some cases only slightly, in others very significantly), it is understandable that no two unions would find economic conditions alike; no two unions would face the same combination of stimulating or retarding influences.

There is no more dramatic evidence of the great differences in union fortunes that can occur simultaneously than that offered by a comparison of the Teamsters Union and the United Mine Workers in the period 1951–1978. During this time, the leading growth union, by a wide margin, was the Teamsters Union, which, having moved from less than 100,000 members in 1933 to 1 million in 1951, continued its spectacular growth (though at a slower rate) to over 1.9 million in 1978. This latter gain of more than 90 percent moved the Teamsters from the rank of third largest to that of largest union in the country.

Meanwhile, the United Mine Workers of America, which, beginning in 1898, was for all but four of forty-four consecutive years the largest union in the United States, and in 1951 was still ranked sixth largest, declined—as a direct result of drastic and lasting reductions in employment in the coal industry—from 600,000 members in 1951 to an estimated 308,000 in 1978, a loss of nearly half of its peak membership.

Available evidence indicates that such diversity, while not generally as dramatic as this, is widespread in the labor movement. According to a recent BLS study, in the period 1960–1976, sixty-five unions reported membership gains, while sixty-six reported losses.[12]

But such data, useful as they are in demonstrating that the overall

[12]U.S. Department of Labor, Bureau of Labor Statistics, *Directory of National Unions and Employee Associations, 1977*, Bulletin 2044, Washington, D.C.: Government Printing Office, 1979, p. 64.

picture conceals widely varying experiences, fail to reveal what is perhaps the most significant and meaningful information of all—the *identity* of the leading unions in the growth stages.

The Growth Unions

Eight unions gained more than 100,000 members each in the decade 1968–1978. The largest *absolute* gains were made by the State, County and Municipal Employees (656,000); the Teachers (335,000); the Service Employees (236,000), and the Retail Clerks (183,000). The Clerks subsequently merged with the Meat Cutters in 1979 to form the United Food and Commercial Workers International Union, whose estimated 1.2 million members made it in 1980 the largest union in the AFL-CIO.

Among these eight unions, the two with the most rapid *rate* of growth were the Teachers (203 percent), and the State, County and Municipal Employees (180 percent). If we label as "growth" unions those that combined the largest absolute gains and the fastest growth, then the State, County, and Municipal Employees and the Teachers, both of which are primarily in the public sector, would rank as the leading growth unions of the past decade.

The Frontier Unions

In addition to the growth unions, there are other unions or associations that are important, irrespective of their size or growth, because they are on the frontier of organized labor activity, penetrating previously unorganized occupations and industries. They are where the venture capital of labor is being invested.

One example of this is union activity among farm workers, which, though "new" in 1962, now appears firmly established, although it is by no means completed, for it remains an area of conflict and controversy, as well as growth.

The farm workers' case is noteworthy because it is essentially an anachronism—a mopping-up operation in the long battle to organize blue-collar workers—at a time when the main thrust of union growth and expansion is among white-collar and professional employees. And it is noteworthy because it provides what amounts to a rerun of the industrial relations history of the 1930's.

In the farm workers, we have a saga of slow and arduous progress, from the establishment of the National Farm Workers Association in 1962, to AFL-CIO organizing committee in 1965, to the United Farm

Workers National Union in 1972; from battles with corporate farms in
the 1960's to struggles with the Teamsters in the 1970's; from virtually
no legal protection to the passage in August 1975 of a California law that
gives farm workers the right to decide by vote what union they want to
represent them—a step that takes the farm workers a step further into
the mainstream of American industrial relations by giving them a right
most industrial workers have had for forty years.

More typical of the frontier of labor organization today is professional sports, where professional athletes first organized for collective
bargaining in the 1960's. Between 1967 and 1969, four such associations were formed—the Major League Umpires Association, the National
Basketball Players Association, the National Football League Players Association, and the National Hockey League Players Association. The Major League Baseball Players Association, founded in the 1950's "at the
urging of owners who feared unionization," has since become independent of the owners, and achieved a written agreement in 1968. Most
readers will recall the 1980 baseball negotiations, and the fact that a
settlement was reached the day of a strike deadline.

Professional employees associations represent a frontier for the
labor movement in another way—in many cases they are not new organizations, but their entry into the collective bargaining process is new.
Thus, such a long-established professional association as the American
Association of University Professors decided as recently as 1972 to turn
to collective bargaining as a way of dealing with professional employment issues (doubtless stimulated by the appearance on college and
university campuses of unions urging faculty members to organize for
collective bargaining). By 1979, the AAUP was devoting more than 25
percent of its national budget to the collective bargaining program, and
had been selected as bargaining representative at 56 institutions—as
against 577 won by either the NEA or the Teachers Union.[13]

The development of faculty unionism was doubtless facilitated by
the decision of the National Labor Relations Board in 1970 to assume
jurisdiction over cases involving nonprofit colleges and universities (the
Cornell case). And now it seems likely that particularly in private colleges and universities, the Supreme Court decision in the Yeshiva case
(which held that the faculty was part of management and that the administration was not required to bargain with them), will impede the growth
of faculty unions.[14]

The past decade has also seen increased union and association
activity in other types of nonprofit institutions—most notably hospitals.
There is no national union for hospital employees as such; instead,

[13]*New York Times*, June 23, 1980.
[14]*New York Times*, February 24, 1980.

organizing activities and campaigns have been undertaken by unions that have taken a special interest in hospital employees. In the East, the spearhead of hospital organizing activities has been a union whose original jurisdiction was primarily in retail drug stores—Local 1199 of the Retail, Wholesale and Department Store Union. In other cases, unions of laundry workers, of cafeteria employees, and of building-service employees have conducted organizing drives among their counterparts in hospitals.

Union activities in the medical and health care field have also been reflected in increased activity among the professional staffs. In addition to nurses, who have long been active in collective bargaining, we have recently witnessed collective action by doctors, residents, and interns.

With the passage in August 1974 of legislation giving the National Labor Relations Board jurisdiction over nonprofit hospitals and nursing homes, we can expect further development of labor organization in the area of health care.

Nor have the arts remained immune to the ferment of union activity. Dancers of the American Ballet Theater have won gains by threatening to strike, and major orchestras and opera companies have been struck—a relatively recent phenomenon, in spite of the fact that the Musicians Union has been prominent in the field for more than half a century.[15]

This brief discussion of the frontiers of the labor movement is necessarily selective rather than inclusive. But it is significant that except for farm labor, the frontiers of organization—as well as the leading growth unions of the decade 1968–1978—are to be found in the service-producing rather than the goods-producing industries. The fact that its newest and strongest growth sectors coincide so closely with the growth sectors of the labor force is a measure of the ability of the labor movement to adapt to a changing industrial environment.

[15]The Metropolitan Opera temporarily cancelled its 1980–1981 season because of a labor dispute, which even an appeal from President Carter failed to resolve. However, the dispute was settled four weeks later and the season's performances continued as scheduled. (See *The New York Times,* September 30 and October 6, 1980.)

Evolving Union Models: A Brief History

The stream of events that make up the history of the American labor movement can be viewed from a number of perspectives. Each is accurate and meaningful, but each is necessarily selective; none can reveal the whole story.

Here we view labor history as a series of conflicts and experiments with various models of organization. Omitting the drama of famous strikes and lockouts and the historic developments in the substantive terms of employment, we concentrate on the no less significant history of labor's search for the organizational models and programs best suited to the needs and objectives of the members and for survival in the American economic and social environment.

The Beginnings

The development of labor organization in the United States is no recent phenomenon; in fact, the appearance of permanent labor unions, roughly comparable to those we know now, occurred less than twenty years after the Declaration of Independence; shoemakers organized in Philadelphia in 1792, carpenters in Boston in 1793, and printers in New York in 1794.[1]

These first unions were made up of craftsmen, who possessed both

[1]The information in this section is drawn largely from two excellent histories of the labor movement: Harry A. Millis and Royal E. Montgomery, *The Economics of Labor,* Vol. III, *Organized Labor* (New York: McGraw-Hill, 1945), pp. 12–73; and Joseph G. Rayback, *A History of American Labor* (New York: Free Press, 1966), pp. 54–184.

the motivation for organization and the bargaining power to make unions effective. But the bargaining techniques of those early unions were rather primitive by today's standards, for give-and-take bargaining and compromise, the essence of bargaining as we know it, were largely unknown. If a union struck for higher wages or a closed shop it was usually on an all or nothing basis—the workers either got their full demands or they got nothing; and more often than not it was nothing. The concept of compromise and negotiation did not develop in practice until after the Civil War. But otherwise, the economic orientation of these early unions was clear enough—they were the unmistakable forerunners of today's business unions.

Organizationally speaking, their chief problem was their great vulnerability to economic recession. Repeatedly, they made real headway during periods of economic expansion and boom. And just as repeatedly, during periods of recession, many—perhaps the majority—simply disintegrated and disappeared. Most of the unions formed in the expansion of 1834–1836, for instance, were wiped out by the panic of 1837, and such major economic slides as those of 1857 and 1873 had similar repercussions.

During these recessions, when the economically oriented trade unions were either disbanded or totally ineffective, workers sought other methods of improving their position; many switched to political activity or joined the ranks of the various reform movements. Labor's first political party, for example, came into existence in 1828 in the midst of a recession, when the Mechanics' Union of Philadelphia was transformed into the Republican Political Association of the Workingmen of Philadelphia; the following year a Working Men's Party was formed in New York City.

Following the panic of 1837, in particular, the uplift and humanitarian sentiments were very strong, and programs ranging from utopian socialism (such as that of the Owenite communities based on the New Harmony experiment) to producers' cooperatives and land reform absorbed much of labor's organizational energies. But, with the return of prosperity, political action and social reform lost their appeal as workers became more interested in the immediate goals of higher wages and better working conditions, and unions were revived or reorganized and the whole cycle began again.

While it vastly oversimplifies the developments on the labor scene between 1800 and 1885, it is fair to say that this dichotomy between political action and economic activity characterized much of the period. Labor vacillated between the two approaches, trying them in different forms and combinations and constantly seeking to strike the proper balance—to find an organizational model and a program which would be the most effective answer to its needs.

Meanwhile, however, the labor movement was gradually developing into something more than just a scattering of isolated and independent local craft unions. Its structure grew vertically as well as horizontally. And, in fact, by 1837, industrial unions as well as craft unions,[2] national unions, and labor federations—almost all the structural forms later developed at one time or another—had made their initial appearance.

In 1827, as part of their drive to secure the ten-hour day in Philadelphia, some fifteen unions formed the Mechanics' Union of Trade Associations—the first city-wide federation of labor unions. By 1836, city federations could be found in some thirteen cities, including most of the major cities on the eastern seaboard.

In 1831, the New England Association of Farmers, Mechanics, and Other Workmen was formed in Providence to organize not just skilled workers but factory operatives as well; basically, it was an early forerunner of industrial unionism—over a century before the founding of the CIO.

Unions in various occupations began to organize along national lines to control competition between unions in different cities. Carpenters, shoemakers, comb-makers, hand-loom weavers, and printers all created national organizations in the period 1834–1837—and all collapsed and disappeared during the depression of 1837.

Even a preliminary attempt at a federation of craft unions was made during this period with the establishment of the National Trades' Union in 1834, the "first federated body in the United States attempting to bring within its membership all local unions, nationals, and city centrals."[3] Like the national unions, this early federation was wiped out in the depression of 1837. But the groundwork had been laid; the seeds of all later organizational forms had been sown.

Beginning shortly before the Civil War, national organizations of craft unions became increasingly numerous and, more important, sufficiently durable for the first time to survive recession. By the end of the 1860's, some thirty national craft unions were active, many of which were to be instrumental in the eventual establishment of the American Federation of Labor.

In 1866, the National Labor Union, a national federation embracing both craft unionists and reform groups, was organized. Although it lasted only six years before being converted into a political party (a party which subsequently collapsed when its presidential candidate withdrew from the election of 1872), in its short existence the National Labor Union set a record for longevity of a national federation. It was indicative of the growing pressure for a national organization which would serve the common interests of labor in different trades and occupations.

---

[2]Craft unions embrace workers of one skill or occupation; industrial unions, workers in a particular industry or group of industries, regardless of occupation. See Chapter 3, p. 48 for fuller discussion.
[3]Mills and Montgomery, *op. cit.*, p. 32.

The Knights of Labor

By all odds the most successful failure among the labor organizations of the nineteenth century was the Noble Order of the Knights of Labor. Founded in 1871 as a secret society, the Knights came into the open as a national organization in 1878, just as a business boom was beginning.

Although they welcomed craft unions into their midst, the Knights regarded pure and simple craft unionism as tending to separate, rather than unify, the working class; they sought to unite all "real" producers— farmers, lower middle class, and wage earners—into one organization. Structurally, the Knights' basic units, the assemblies, generally brought skilled and unskilled workers together, a fact which proved increasingly distasteful to the craftsmen, if for no other reason than that it interfered with their bargaining effectiveness. And organizationally, the Knights were centralized rather than decentralized, with no provision for national unions; their rules, in fact, prohibited national trade associations. So far as a program was concerned, they were opposed in principle to strikes and were more interested in reform and education than in immediate economic gains.

The Knights, in short, were the polar opposite of the craft-union model of organization—indeed, theirs may be considered a primitive model of industrial unionism, without the business-union approach of today's industrial unions.

Both the rise and fall of the Knights of Labor were spectacular. In 1883, five years after they came into the open, the Knights claimed barely 50,000 members. But in 1884 and 1885 recession struck, and as the unions suffered their customary decline the workers turned "from the empty larder of business unionism to the attractive menu of an uplift association."[4] And when the Knights, successful in spite of themselves, won a strike in 1885 against Jay Gould, at that time "perhaps the most powerful capitalist in the United States,"[5] 600,000 members joined in a single year.

In 1886, at their peak strength, the Knights had nearly 700,000 members—not much by today's standards, but an all-time high at that point in history. Yet, two years later, the Knights' membership had fallen to 220,000; and by 1890, only four years after reaching its apogee, the Knights' membership had dwindled to 100,000 and the fledgling AFL, founded at the peak of the Knights' strength, had already won the allegiance of a majority of the trade unions. The Knights had been a true meteor on the labor horizon—a brilliant flash that burned out.

[4]*Ibid.*, p. 63.
[5]*Loc. cit.*

The sudden disintegration of the Knights was due to a combination of circumstances. Among other things, they had been hurt by the Haymarket riot of May 1886, precipitated when a bomb was thrown at police trying to disperse a protest meeting against "police brutality" during a strike at the McCormick Reaper plant in Chicago. In the ensuing riot, several persons were fatally wounded and many others injured. Although not implicated in the affair, the Knights undoubtedly suffered from the widespread antilabor sentiment and fear that Haymarket provoked—fear so great that one prominent Chicago businessman, building a new house in 1890, installed a button marked "MOB" which he could punch to call the police.[6] Without a business union base to fall back on, the Knights were harder hit than their competitor, the AFL.

The American Federation of Labor and Craft Unionism

One of the key elements in the decline and fall of the Knights was the appearance of the American Federation of Labor, which, when founded in 1886, benefited substantially from the dissatisfaction of the craft unions with the "one big union" approach and the consequent failure of the Knights to give greater attention to their particular needs.

The AFL,[7] in fact, was both a response and a reaction to the Knights of Labor: a response in that it was organized precisely when the discontent of the craft unionists offered a golden opportunity for an organization designed to meet their needs; and a reaction in that the phenomenal growth of the Knights, especially in 1886, had been partly at the expense of the existing craft unions. The Knights had not been hesitant to raid the craft unions, and the formation of the AFL may be seen in part as a defensive measure by the craft unions.

As we examine the structure and policies of the AFL (the most successful of their kind thus far devised), it should be emphasized that they were not simply the result of a stroke of inspired genius on the part of Samuel Gompers and his fellow union leaders in the AFL. Rather, it should be clear that the structure and policies of the AFL were the fruits of over fifty years of trial and error in the American labor movement—Gompers and company knew well the lessons of those fifty years' experience and applied them in creating the new federation.

---

[6]Irving Bernstein, "Union Growth and Structural Cycles," *Proceedings,* Industrial Relations Research Association, 1954, p. 205 n.

[7]For many generations, the letters "AFL" (or "A. F. of L.," as it called itself) referred, not to a football league, but to the American Federation of Labor, a union league, as it were.

A word about Gompers is in order, nevertheless. Chosen to be the first president of the American Federation of Labor in 1886 at the age of 36, Gompers remained president until 1924 with only one interruption—in 1894, when he was out of office for a year after a close defeat at the convention.

Gompers came to the AFL from the Cigar Makers Union and, needless to say, was a staunch defender of the craft-union point of view. It has been suggested that the chief reason he was chosen to head the AFL was that no full-time union leader would accept the post in an organization so lacking in promise as the young AFL.[8] Yet, when he died four decades later, Gompers had left an indelible mark, not only on the AFL but on the labor movement as a whole. Gompers' genius, as we have suggested, lay not in his ability to invent new approaches and policies but rather in his understanding of the strengths and weaknesses of the Federation and in his skill in making the most of them.

The founding of the American Federation of Labor in 1886 not only falls roughly halfway between the appearance of the first American unions in the 1790's and this writing (1980), but in a very real sense it marks the beginning of modern unionism as we know it today.

Like others before it, the AFL represented a particular model of unionism—craft unionism—and it offered this model as an alternative and an improvement upon models that had gone before. It expected its craft federation model to correct some of the shortcomings of previous models and to provide an adequate solution to problems which previous models had found insurmountable.

In retrospect, we can say that a notable feature of the craft-union model of labor organization, as pursued and practiced by the AFL and its affiliated national unions, was that it was the first to survive the rigors of business fluctuations without simply disintegrating and having to start over. In short, the AFL model was the first to achieve permanence, regardless of economic conditions. Indeed, while it had many shortcomings, as we will see subsequently, the AFL maintained an unbroken and continuous existence for nearly seventy years, from 1886 until its merger with the CIO in 1955. This alone gives the AFL a unique place in American labor history.

It seems quite likely that it was skillful management as much as the inherent advantages of craft unionism that accounted for the great success of the craft-union model in the hands of the AFL. The managerial formula for the administration of the AFL was clearly defined by Samuel Gompers, its first president, and adhered to with little variation until the rise of the CIO and the passage of the Wagner Act modified its impact. Central to Gompers' administrative formula were two basic pol-

---

[8]Philip Taft, *The A. F. of L. in the Time of Gompers* (New York: Harper & Row, 1957), p. 39.

icies: first, that the national unions which belonged to the AFL were to be guaranteed "trade autonomy"; and second, that they were to be afforded "exclusive jurisdiction" over their particular craft or other occupation.

To use modern business terminology, the promise of "trade autonomy" meant that decision making was to be decentralized, with the national unions retaining the ultimate authority to make decisions for themselves. Although it applied to all activities of the national unions, economic and political alike, this decentralization was particularly important when it came to the unions' main function, collective bargaining, for it meant (among other things) that, on the union side, collective-bargaining decisions would be made by those best equipped by knowledge and experience to know the problems involved—the officers of the union in the occupation or trade—rather than by some general officer from the Federation offices in Washington.

Similarly, the policy of exclusive jurisdiction was the labor union counterpart of the exclusive business franchise or dealership. By granting the Carpenters Union, for example, exclusive jurisdiction in its field, the AFL recognized its sole authority to organize carpenters (and the sole right of members of the Carpenters Union to do "carpenters' work"). Thus, it was protected against possible competition from other unions by assurances that no other unions would be given overlapping jurisdiction, and no competitor (if one already existed) would be recognized by the AFL. That this policy proved to be harder to administer and enforce than to enunciate was not entirely the fault of Gompers or the AFL; the problem, as we shall see later, was that changing technology kept upsetting the neat divisions of power that the AFL laid out, forcing the constant re-examination of the question of jurisdiction over occupations and jobs that had not existed when the original charters were issued.

Taken together, the policies of autonomy and exclusive jurisdiction proved remarkably successful in attracting organizations to the new federation, and it is not hard to understand why—they gave the national unions a great deal of freedom.

Autonomy ensured their freedom from intervention by the Federation. It should be emphasized, of course, that it was not a question of the Federation offering the national unions a new and attractive advantage. The AFL did not *confer* autonomy on the national unions; the plain fact was that the national unions *had* autonomy; they were already independent decision-making organizations. The Federation's strategy was simply to *recognize* their autonomy, realizing that the only way national unions could be induced to join the Federation was by the pledge of hard and fast constitutional guarantees that their independence and autonomy would not be abridged. The AFL was in the position of the United Nations in its early years—trying to attract membership with assurances that sovereignty would not be impaired by joining it.

Exclusive jurisdiction, by giving a national union monopolistic rights to represent the workers in a particular occupation, gave it a measure of freedom from competition from other national unions (whose predatory instincts had been revealed on many occasions). One disadvantage, which at the time of the founding of the AFL might well have seemed remote, was that while exclusive jurisdiction fenced competing unions *out,* it also fenced its possessor *in* and limited its activities to a specific area or occupation.[9] At any rate, at the time, the benefits appeared to outweigh the costs. The national unions retained their independence in handling the key union function of collective bargaining and gained protection against competition.

A third key point in the AFL formula was insistence on organization by crafts or trades—the organization of skilled workers, with a separate union for each separate skill or occupational specialty. Economically speaking, the distinctive characteristic of a "skill" is that it is the product of relatively long training. The skilled craftsmen are thus specialists who tend to be both in relatively short supply and, because of their ability, difficult to replace. To be blunt about it, the fact that they are hard to replace gives them great leverage in making demands on their employers; this was and is the prime source of their bargaining power.

In addition, however, the economic power inherent in their skill was enhanced by the organizational structure adopted by the AFL. Establishing a separate union for each distinct craft or skill—the carpenters, the bricklayers, or the plumbers, for example—gave the workers the advantages of *organizational* as well as *individual* specialization. And because all the members of a single craft union shared a common skill, the problem of formulating union demands was simplified—conflicts of interest *within* the union tended to be minimized and *internal* bargaining in the formulation of union demands was reduced. But undoubtedly the most important advantage of such organizational specialization was that it enabled the unions to focus sharply their economic power so as to bring the greatest possible pressure upon the employers. As Chamberlain has pointed out: "One advantage of the craft union structure is the key position which skilled workers frequently play in an enterprise, coupled with the relatively low wage bill which they entail. A strike of a handful of powerhouse employees may close down an entire plant, involving the employer in a substantial cost of disagreeing on their terms, whereas because of their small number the

---

[9]For an analysis of this point, see Marten S. Estey, "Trends in Concentration of Union Membership, 1897–1962," *Quarterly Journal of Economics,* Vol. LXXX (August 1966), pp. 354–355.

cost of agreement may be negligible in comparison, even if they demand an 'outrageous' pay increase."[10]

Once the Federation chose to emphasize economic rather than political or other objectives, the craft-union structure was the logical one, for in the economic environment of the late nineteenth century, it was clearly the way to maximize economic gains.

Since the bargaining power of the craft union appeared to be the mechanism through which economic gains could be maximized, it was only sound management to concentrate the unions' limited resources there, where they would do the most good. Accordingly, it was an integral part of the AFL formula to emphasize collective bargaining as the primary union function and to give it top priority as the means for achieving union objectives.

The priority given to collective bargaining, of course, had a number of consequences. It meant, in the first place, minimizing the efforts devoted to political activity. It meant a long-run shift of power from the local union to the national union. Most significant of all, it meant that the AFL had chosen business unionism and the path of accommodation and compromise with management.

Closely related to the preceding principles was the AFL view of the role of unions in politics. The craft (or trade) union majority in the Federation, adhering to a philosophy that had been expressed as early as 1872, insisted that the AFL should maintain a nonpartisan political stance, avoiding either entangling alliances with existing political parties or "independent" political action in the form of a separate labor party.

This opposition to partisan political commitment reflected a variety of factors: (1) the conviction that the labor movement should concentrate its energies on collective bargaining and not risk dissipating them in political activity as the Knights of Labor had; (2) a long-standing craft union fear that political ties were more likely to divide than to unify the labor movement, for though workers might be united in their concern for economic improvement at work, it was apparent that on political issues their interests and loyalties were as diverse as those of any other segment of the population; and (3) a realistic recognition that a uniform, Federation-wide political stand, which a partisan political position would imply, was not compatible with the policy of national union autonomy upon which the whole administration of the Federation may be said to have been based.

But its opposition to *partisan* politics did not mean that the Federation sought to remain aloof from politics. Far from it; from the outset, Gompers and his fellow trade-unionists saw that certain problems de-

---

[10]Neil W. Chamberlain and James W. Kuhn, *Collective Bargaining,* 2nd ed. (New York: McGraw-Hill, 1965), p. 174.

manded legislative solutions. The AFL, accordingly, lobbied for specific legislation as needed and adopted the policy of "reward your friends and punish your enemies." This meant that political judgments should be based on the candidates and, more specifically, on their record in matters of labor interest, rather than on their party labels. This technique had the particular advantage, furthermore, of enhancing labor's political bargaining power.

In short, the AFL under Gompers' leadership was not apolitical; it simply chose pressure-group politics in preference to party politics, using its political power to serve its immediate self-interest, as is the usual practice of economic interest groups. Unlike many pressure groups, however, the AFL preferred to put primary reliance upon economic activity for achieving its objectives and to relegate political activity to second place.

Somewhat paradoxically, perhaps, Gompers also advocated what was known in labor circles as "voluntarism," opposing government intervention to improve living or working standards directly by legislation on the grounds that if such benefits were provided by the government it would interfere with the unions' role as the source of such gains, and the workers would therefore be less likely to join unions for self-improvement. On these grounds, Gompers found himself in league with employers in opposing government intervention into labor problems.

All in all, Gompers' formula for administering the AFL was remarkably business-like. It recognized the practical values of monopoly (exclusive jurisdiction) and of specialization (separate unions for each craft); it concentrated on decision making at the plant level or the firm level and opposed centralized decision making or standard setting by government. It is no accident that the AFL is identified with the concept of business unionism.

Taken together, these policies proved remarkably successful in attracting unions and members into the new federation. From 1897 to 1904, for example, when union membership rose even more rapidly than in the expansion of the late 1930's, AFL unions accounted for 1,400,000 new members, or 85 percent of the 1,625,700 increase in total union membership.[11]

Even more indicative of the young AFL's organizational vigor is the fact that between 1897 and 1904 it issued a total of 92 charters, with the result that the number of its affiliated unions more than doubled, rising to a total of 120 in 1904. This figure was not surpassed for over fifty years, until the AFL-CIO merger in 1955. By 1904, 85 percent of all national unions in the United States were affiliated with the AFL.[12]

---

[11]Data from Leo Wolman, *Ebb and Flow in Trade Unionism* (New York: National Bureau of Economic Research, Inc., 1936), p. 138.
[12]Estey, *op. cit.,* p. 353.

After 1904, growth was less dramatic. By 1914, AFL membership had just passed the 2-million mark. Rising briefly to 4 million, AFL strength, like that of other unions, then declined gradually throughout the 1920's and by 1933 had fallen back to less than 2.5 million.

Nor has the craft-union model lost its validity today. Despite the vast changes in the industrial environment and in technology, and the structural upheaval in organized labor in the 1930's, the craft unions are still a major influence in the labor movement. The Carpenters and the Machinists, for example, ranked among the ten largest unions in 1897 (the Carpenters ranked second, the Machinists ninth) and were *still* among the top ten unions in 1978 (seventh and sixth, respectively). And membership in the construction industry, perhaps the heart of the craft-union group in the AFL-CIO, accounts for some 2.8 million members, making it the second largest industrial group in the labor movement.

The CIO and Industrial Unionism

The craft-union model of labor organization, as embodied in the American Federation of Labor and its affiliated national unions, prevailed virtually unchallenged for half a century—from the founding of the AFL in 1886 until 1935. But in 1935, the pre-eminence of the craft union as the type of organization best adapted to cope with the American economic and social environment was abruptly challenged by the establishment of a new organization which advocated a significantly different model of unionism.

The new organization was the CIO—the Committee for Industrial Organization—and its model was *industrial unionism,* whose distinguishing characteristic is membership based upon employment in an *industry,* regardless of occupation or skill, rather than upon employment in a particular skilled occupation, as in the craft union.

The cue for the launching of the CIO was appropriately dramatic— physical combat between two men who personified the differences between craft and industrial unionism.

At the 1935 convention of the AFL, during a discussion of industrial unionism in the rubber industry, "Big Bill" Hutcheson, president of the Carpenters Union and a staunch defender of the craft union position, raised a point of order to object that the industrial union issue had already been settled in favor of the craft unions.

John L. Lewis, president of the United Mine Workers and leader of the industrial-union forces within the AFL, snorted scornfully, "This thing of raising points of order all the time on minor delegates is rather small potatoes."

"I was raised on small potatoes, that's why I'm so small," shot back Hutcheson, one of the tallest and heaviest men in the convention.[13]

"Well, then, it's about time you were mashed," Lewis said, striking Hutcheson, and the two tangled and fell to the floor.

This clash marked the beginning of what proved to be a twenty-year division in the mainstream of the American labor movement. On November 9, 1935, Lewis, representing the Mine Workers, plus the presidents of seven other unions in the industrial union bloc, met and established the Committee for Industrial Organization, to encourage the organization of the unorganized workers in mass-production industries on an industrial basis.

Summoned before the AFL Executive Council for a hearing on charges of ignoring the decision of the convention and, worse, of committing the capital offense of dual unionism, Lewis and his cohorts in the CIO refused to attend. Told to disband the CIO or be suspended, they ignored the order. With that, the break was complete and the CIO, which later formalized its independence by changing its name to the Congress—instead of "Committee"—of Industrial Organizations, was on its own.

The contrast between the first years of the AFL and those of the CIO is as the contrast between night and day. In its first years, the AFL caused hardly a ripple outside the labor movement; public attention was still riveted on the Knights of Labor. The activities of the newly formed CIO, on the other hand, not only attracted national attention, but were notable even in an era crammed with notable events.

The CIO's efforts to break into the mass-production industries were dramatic, to say the least. Indeed, as one writer put it, they comprised "the most remarkable episode in the annals of American labor."[14]

Within a single three-week period in early 1937, the CIO brought to terms the largest corporations in both the auto and the steel industries, and by thus penetrating to the very heart of the mass-production industries, paved the way for their subsequent, virtually complete organization. "The entire social structure of the country, its basic power relationships, were altered fundamentally . . . the United States had suddenly been propelled into the ranks of those nations in which the voice of organized labor counted."[15]

Symbolically, the CIO's first great success came in the auto industry, then, as now, the epitome of the mass-production industries. On February 11, 1937, after nearly six weeks of "the most critical labor conflict

---

[13]*Proceedings* of the Fifty-Fifth Annual Convention of the American Federation of Labor, 1935, p. 727. Lewis' alleged reply to Hutcheson, as quoted here, is omitted from this Report.

[14]Walter Galenson, "1937: The Turning Point for American Labor," Reprint No. 120 (Berkeley: Institute of Industrial Relations, University of California, 1959), p. 117.

[15]*Loc. cit.*

of the 1930's,"[16] General Motors, the largest of the big three automobile manufacturers, signed an agreement recognizing the United Auto Workers as the bargaining agent for its members.

And on March 2, while industry was still reeling from the shock of the General Motors agreement, the United States Steel Corporation, the bellwether of the steel industry, on its own initiative, and with no advance indications of its intention, signed an agreement with the Steel Workers Organizing Committee, through negotiations between Myron Taylor, chairman of the board of the corporation, and John L. Lewis.

As Walter Galenson has written:

> ... even the recognition of the United Automobile Workers Union by General Motors a week earlier did not have the impact of the steel settlement, since the GM agreement had been reached after a long and bitter sit-down strike, and with the most severe form of pressure exercised by the federal and state governments. Here, on the contrary, there had been virtually no government intervention and no industrial strife. The agreement was worked out by the parties themselves on a voluntary basis."[17]

The two cases present an interesting contrast. Originally chartered by the AFL in 1935, the United Auto Workers was dissatisfied at the restrictions imposed by the AFL and switched its affiliation to the CIO in July 1936. Although aided and abetted by Lewis and the CIO, the Auto Workers was from the first an aggressively independent union, unwilling to take orders from anyone in or out of the labor movement. The weapon with which the UAW forced General Motors to capitulate was the controversial sit-down strike, a forerunner of the civil-rights techniques of the mid-1960's. Instead of the customary refusal to *come* to work, the sit-down strike was a refusal to *leave* work. In a sit-down strike, the workers occupied or seized a plant or factory and could be dislodged only by force. Subsequently declared illegal, and virtually abandoned even before the Supreme Court decision, the sit-down strikes of 1936 and 1937 were a key tactic in winning the General Motors strike— though intervention by both President Roosevelt and the Governor of Michigan was not insignificant.

The unprecedented success of the General Motors strike paved the way for the UAW to make rapid strides in the auto industry. Although UAW membership on the eve of the General Motors strike is not known, by June 1937, six months after the beginning of the strike, the union had won agreements with all the major producers except Ford (which

---

[16]Walter Galenson, *The CIO Challenge to the AFL, A History of the American Labor Movement, 1935–1941* (Cambridge: Harvard University Press, 1960), p. 134. This is the authoritative study of the rise of the CIO and its constituent unions.
[17]*Ibid.*, p. 93.

was not unionized until 1941) and with many of the parts manufacturers, and claimed a dues-paying membership of 520,000.

And even though the sharp recession of 1937 brought the expansion abruptly to a halt, with unemployment cutting heavily into membership, the fact remains that, at the end of 1937, before it was even three years old, the UAW had catapulted into the position of fourth largest union in the United States.

In the summer of 1936, the CIO had established the Steel Workers Organizing Committee (SWOC), financed it with a $500,000 initial grant (according to one source, more money than had ever been pledged for a single organizing campaign), and provided its officers, Philip Murray and David J. McDonald, both of whom were later to become presidents of the Steelworkers Union. In short, the SWOC, unlike the UAW, was the creature of the CIO.

Following the peaceful capitulation of US Steel, the SWOC, too, made rapid progress and, by June 1937, claimed agreements with 142 steel companies and a membership of 376,000. But from here on, the path of the SWOC proved considerably more rocky than that of the UAW.

In May and June 1937, in efforts to expand its position in the steel industry, the SWOC struck the plants of the so-called "Little Steel" companies. In vivid contrast to the peaceful victory in US Steel, the Little Steel strikes were the scene of bitter and unsuccessful battles. In "the Memorial Day incident" alone, 10 people were killed and 125 others injured. And when the Little Steel strikes were closely followed by the recession of 1937, the expansion of unionism in the steel industry was effectively halted, not to be renewed until the upheaval of World War II revived both the economic conditions in the steel industry and a climate favorable to unionism.

The CIO successes in both the auto and steel industries were by all odds its most impressive accomplishments. Quite aside from the speed with which they were carried out and the fact that they constituted penetration of what had been virtually unorganized industries, they demonstrated that industrial unionism would work where craft unionism had failed.

The CIO also penetrated other major industries in 1937—electrical and radio manufacturing, rubber, men's and women's clothing, textiles, meat packing, petroleum, and the maritime industry.

By the end of 1937, 33 national unions or organizing committees had affiliated with the CIO. Its total membership, according to recent estimates, was approximately 2 million, as compared with the venerable AFL's 3 million, and it could claim five of the ten largest unions.

At the end of the 1937 recession (one of the sharpest the country had ever experienced), the CIO was concentrating its efforts in the durable-goods industries. Although the recession had an especially severe impact on these industries, bringing CIO expansion to a grinding halt, the union's growth was resumed as business activity accelerated shortly before our entry into World War II.

In 1941, the organization of both the steel and auto industries was completed—steel by virtue of an NLRB order to the recalcitrant Little Steel companies to comply with the Wagner Act, and the auto industry as a result of the decision of Henry Ford to deal with the UAW.

Wartime expansion, as usual, further stimulated the growth of unions, both CIO and AFL. CIO membership by 1944 was 3.9 million, more than double its strength in 1937. In 1953, during the Korean War, the CIO reached its all-time peak, with nearly 5 million members, of whom over a million each were in the auto and steel industries, and a quarter million each in the clothing, textile, communications, and electrical industries. When, in late 1937 and 1938, the CIO fumbled its drive for expansion, the AFL was galvanized into action and picked up the ball the CIO had dropped. In the course of its counterattack, the AFL recaptured its position as the dominant federation (if, in fact, it had ever lost it) by increasing its membership from 3 million in 1937 to 6.8 million in 1944. And while the CIO expansion had pretty much leveled off by 1947, the AFL continued to grow, from 8.5 million in 1947 to 10.5 million in 1955, at the time of the merger.

But the recovery of the AFL in no way indicated that the lessons of the CIO experience were ignored. Instead, many of the AFL's major unions abandoned the strict-craft union model and proceeded to adapt themselves to attract the semi-skilled worker, just as the CIO had. The rapid expansion of the Teamsters, Carpenters, and Machinists was due in large part to just such adaptation. Industrial unionism, whether under the aegis of the CIO or the AFL, had come to stay.

In weighing the factors which went into the emergence and success of the CIO, the leadership role of John L. Lewis, "perhaps the greatest entrepreneur of American Labor organizations," looms large. The stormy petrel of American unionism—who stepped down as president of the CIO only five years after he had founded it, who then took his union back to the AFL only to break with it again in 1947 and become independent of either federation, and who, in late 1941, less than six weeks before Pearl Harbor, could refuse a request from the President of the United States to send striking coal miners back to work while negotiations continued—was, as one writer put it, "as tough as the most antiunion employer; he possessed great administrative talents and had a flair for dramatizing himself and his cause . . . above all he was willing to play for high stakes. Lewis was very much in the tradition of the industrial tycoons who had built American industry, only he operated on the other side of the fence."[18]

Although the successful creation of industrial unions and the CIO can be attributed to Lewis' shrewd sense of timing and his vigorous and imaginative tactics in taking advantage of the stimulus of the Wagner Act, economic conditions, and the shift in public policy toward labor, made the circumstances ripe for a new form of labor organization.

Half a century earlier, when the AFL was founded, the United States was still in the process of transition from an agricultural to a manufacturing economy. Large economic enterprises had already appeared, to be sure (witness the Sherman Antitrust Act of 1890, designed to prevent excessive concentration of economic power), but much of what we know as the modern mass-production industries had not yet been developed.

In 1886, there was no automobile industry. The United States Steel Corporation was yet to be organized. The rubber industry was small. There were no radios. Plants were smaller, and no business employed workers in the numbers that are common today.

By 1935, on the other hand, the development of the mass-production industries such as automobiles, steel, rubber, and radios, had produced a situation which inadvertently gave to the unskilled and semi-skilled a source of economic power unknown when the skilled workers were first being organized by the AFL. That source of power, very simply, was the sheer power of numbers. While the skilled worker had long relied on the scarcity factor to make him difficult to replace and to give him bargaining power, the unskilled worker, individually or in small groups, was readily replaceable. But when we find 40,000 workers employed in a single establishment, as was the case at the Ford Motor Company's Rouge plant in Detroit in 1935, then it makes little difference whether they are unskilled, semi-skilled or skilled—if they strike, their numbers alone make their prompt and effective replacement virtually impossible. In short, the sheer size of the modern mass-production enterprise provided the unskilled and semi-skilled workers with the power to back up their demands for improved wages, hours, and working conditions.

In 1937, the workers in the mass-production industries had economic power, a newly favorable legal climate, and strong leadership. Only one additional ingredient was needed—motivation. And they had it. In fact, "The principal ingredient which went into the success of the 1937 campaign was the strength of organizational sentiment among American workers," Galenson claims, adding: "Their belief in the efficiency of capitalism was all but destroyed by the shattering experience

---

[18]Galenson, "1937: The Turning Point for American Labor," *op. cit.,* p. 112.

of the depression. It was not low wages which were fundamentally at the root of their dissatisfaction, for the CIO made its greatest headway in relatively high-wage industries. What workers rebelled against was the insecurity of their employment, the arbitrary character of management decisions affecting their lives, and the speeding up of work by companies seeking desperately to prevent operating losses."[19]

The Expulsion of Communist Unions[20]

Just as the AFL had been bothered at one time or another with the problem of corruption and racketeering in its affiliated unions, the CIO faced the problem of Communist influence in its affiliates. And both federations faced essentially the same problem in trying to cope with them—the fact that the autonomy of the national unions which belonged to them prevented direct intervention to solve the problem.

The origins of the problem of Communist influence in the CIO and its affiliates are complex, but two reasons for this problem deserve mention here. First, long before its successful adoption as the organizational model of the CIO, industrial unionism had been advocated as the proper solution for organizing the unskilled, principally by left-wing groups in the labor movement. While this in no way means that industrial unionists were all left-wingers or radicals, it was true that this long espousal by the left meant that when the industrial unions were established, the left-wing element tended to gravitate toward them in preference to the AFL unions.

Second, it is generally believed that John L. Lewis, who was by no means naive about them, knowingly utilized the Communists in the great CIO organizing drives, confident that he could control them.

But after the CIO's organization of the mass-production industries had reached its peak, and after the urgent demands of World War II had passed, it became clear that the Communists had become a powerful influence in unions whose membership represented perhaps one-third of total CIO membership. And, as the end of the war brought our alliance with Russia to an end, the divergence of interests between the Communist-dominated unions and the rest of the CIO became prominent.

As a result, the CIO in 1949 and 1950 expelled a total of eleven unions for following the program of the Communist Party in preference to the objectives of the CIO. The combined membership of these eleven

---

[19]*Ibid.*, p. 110.

[20]For the material on which this section is based, see Arthur J. Goldberg, *AFL-CIO, Labor United* (New York: McGraw-Hill, 1956), pp. 173–187.

unions was approximately 1 million members—nearly one-fifth of the total CIO strength at that time. Most of these members were subsequently recaptured by the CIO, in part by new unions chartered to replace those that had been expelled.

The expelled unions, on the other hand, fared poorly. By 1978, only two of the eleven (with a combined membership of 221,000) were still functioning as separate entities—the International Longshoremen's and Warehousemen's Union (ILWU) and the United Electrical, Radio and Machine Workers of America (UE).[21]

The impact of their expulsion from the CIO and the generally adverse effects of continued prosperity on the appeals of the Communist program appear to have brought Communist influence in the labor movement to a new low.

Changing Union Policy

The rise of the CIO and the industrial unions was not the only significant change in the structure and program of the labor movement to occur during the 1930's. The principle of exclusive jurisdiction, one of the pillars of AFL policy since the 1880's, was permanently modified. Two things account for this breakdown. Obviously enough, one was the creation of the CIO—with its establishment, the AFL no longer was the exclusive *source* of jurisdiction, and instead there were *two* major jurisdiction-granting federations, with no mechanism for preventing rivalry, competition, and overlapping jurisdictions.

Consequently, for nearly twenty years there were two auto workers unions—the UAW-AFL and its better known rival, the UAW-CIO. Today, there are three national unions whose primary interest is in the electrical industry—the IBEW, the IUE, and the UE. The list could be expanded substantially, but the point is clear: exclusive jurisdiction is a thing of the past.

The other major factor to affect the concept of exclusive jurisdiction ws the Wagner Act of 1935. By giving the *workers* (through the secret-ballot election) the power to choose the union to which they would belong, the law in fact gave *them,* rather than the AFL or the CIO, the power to determine which union had jurisdiction over them. Under these circumstances, no union could be sure of exclusive jurisdiction.

The other pillar of AFL policy, the autonomy of the national unions, remained little changed. Although the CIO had created, staffed, and financed an international union—such as the Steelworkers—it gener-

---

[21]The American Communications Association merged with the Teamsters in October 1966, and the Mine, Mill and Smelter Workers affiliated with the Steelworkers in February 1967.

ally recognized, as the AFL did, the basic fact that the national unions *were* autonomous organizations.

Labor's political posture also changed significantly during the 1930's, in part in response to the flow of social legislation and the increased role of the government itself, in part because of the political interests of the CIO (which as early as 1936, through Labor's Non-Partisan League, spent over a million dollars in the campaign to re-elect President Roosevelt), and in part because the great growth of union membership meant a corresponding growth in labor's political impact.

Perhaps the CIO's most lasting contribution to organized labor's increased political involvement came in 1943, with the establishment of the Political Action Committee—the PAC. Essentially, the PAC was designed to get at the grassroots, to inform the individual union member and to get him out to vote; it carried union political activity down to the precinct and the ward levels. Today, the techniques of the PAC are to be found in the AFL-CIO Committee on Political Education, or COPE, and are emulated as well—ironic as it seems—in the recently established corporate PAC's.

Although organized labor cannot "deliver" the vote, since they have no sure means of controlling it, it is obvious that an organization with 15.6 million members (the AFL-CIO in 1978) is going to pack more political punch than one of less than 3 million (the AFL in 1933). And while the AFL-CIO still maintains an officially nonpartisan position—it has traditionally sought to "elect liberals to Congress regardless of party affiliation"—in practice, nonpartisanship has generally led to the support of Democratic rather than Republican candidates. That the AFL-CIO is no political appendage of the Democratic party was amply demonstrated by its refusal to support George McGovern, the Democratic candidate for President in the 1972 elections (thus contributing directly to Nixon's re-election); nevertheless, their relationship is a close one, and organized labor plays an important role in Democratic party councils.

The AFL-CIO Merger

The big reunion between the AFL and the CIO took place on December 5, 1955, when, after a twenty-year separation, they merged into a single federation, the American Federation of Labor and Congress of Industrial Organizations. The new federation consisted of 138 national and international unions (108 from the AFL and 30 from the CIO), with a combined membership of 16.1 million (10.9 million from the AFL and 5.2 from the CIO).

Although efforts to heal the breach between the AFL and the CIO had begun almost immediately after the original split in 1935, certain specific factors appear to have contributed significantly to the actual consummation of the merger in 1955.

One contributing factor may be described as political—the passage of the Taft-Hartley Act in 1947. Both the AFL and the CIO were deeply disturbed by the Taft-Hartley Act; both roundly denounced it as a "slave-labor act" (because it provided for injunctions to force strikers back to work during "national emergency strikes"); and both vowed retaliation at the polls against its chief sponsor, Senator Taft of Ohio. When, to the chagrin of the two federations, the combined effect of their separate political campaigns against Senator Taft proved fruitless and he was re-elected, the question whether organized labor could continue to afford the luxury of rivalry at the price of political impotence became too persistent to overlook. The Taft-Hartley experience, in short, strongly suggested the practical necessity of combining forces if organized labor were to avert further legislative and political reverses.

Equally pressing, particularly from the CIO viewpoint, was the loss of membership it incurred as a result of its expulsion of the eleven national unions during 1949–1950 on charges of Communist domination. Collectively, these expulsions cost the CIO nearly 1 million members, or close to 20 percent of its membership at that time. And quite aside from this loss, the fact was painfully apparent to the CIO that it had achieved only half the membership of the AFL. To be businesslike, it was evident that a merger of the two federations might effect substantial economies of scale, if only by eliminating duplication of effort and improving coordination.

Closely related to this was another problem of great concern to both the AFL and the CIO—the problem of "raiding," in which one union attempted to gain members not by organizing the unorganized worker but by attacking other unions and pirating their membership. Widely practiced by both AFL and CIO unions, the raids not only cost the labor movement millions of dollars that could better have been spent for expansion, but, as a joint AFL-CIO study revealed, had been largely futile as well.

The study's analysis of National Labor Relations Board election results for the years 1951–1952 showed just how fruitless raiding actually was. As a result of more than 1,200 attempted raids, involving over 365,000 workers, only 62,000 workers changed unions. And since these changes were largely offsetting *exchanges,* the net result was that AFL unions gained the meager total of 8,000 members—less than 2 percent of the number involved!

Accordingly, in December 1953, as a first concrete step toward merger, officials of both the AFL and the CIO signed a "no-raiding agreement" which was subsequently signed by 65 AFL and 29 CIO national unions. As Arthur Goldberg, former Ambassador to the UN and former general counsel to the United Steelworkers has remarked, "The lesson to be drawn from that tabulation was so clear and the figures so overwhelming in their demonstration of the futility of raiding, that agreement at least in principle that it would be desirable to ban all raids between unions affiliated with the two federations was almost impossible to resist."[22]

Finally, and probably most important in the timing of the merger, was the change in the top leadership of both the AFL and the CIO. When the CIO split off from the AFL in 1935, the president of the AFL was William Green, and that of the CIO was John L. Lewis. In 1940, Lewis stepped down as president of the CIO (having promised to do so if President Roosevelt were re-elected) and was succeeded in that post by Philip Murray, his close associate in the United Mine Workers. Thus, both Green and Murray had been deeply involved in the tumultuous events surrounding the formation of the CIO, and while both may well have seen the need of recreating a single federation, neither could comfortably participate in such a move except on face-saving terms. As a result, so long as Green and Murray were at the helm they constituted a formidable barrier to the compromises and concessions necessary to bring a merger to reality.

In 1952 the situation changed. First Green and then Murray died—both less than a month after the election, on November 4, 1952, of the first Republican administration since Hoover's. Whether the prospect of a return to Republicanism was more than the two old Democrats could stand we cannot tell. Their successors, George Meany of the AFL and Walter Reuther of the CIO, while ardent supporters of their organizations, had played less critical roles in the original drama and could move forward toward the merger without a sense of personal surrender.

Even at that, the final negotiations for the merger took another three years, and it was not until December 1955 that the merger agreement was finally signed.

It is noteworthy that, at the time, the merger was the cause of widespread apprehension among the business community. The merger, it was reasoned, created a huge labor monopoly, half again as big as the AFL had been alone, and put it at the disposal of a single man, George Meany, the president of the merged organizations. And, thus, Meany, so it seemed to the alarmists, simply had to pick up a phone to call out not 10 million workers but 16 million who, at one fell swoop, would bring the nation's economy to a grinding halt and put it at the mercy of Meany and his cohorts.

[22]Goldberg, *op. cit.,* p. 77.

This fearful prospect, of course, was groundless, for in the newly merged AFL-CIO, as in the former separate federations, each national and international union was to remain completely autonomous, with sole control over its actions. In fact, therefore, Meany had no more control over the Auto Workers the day *after* the merger than he did the day before, because even though the Auto Workers had become a part of the new federation, it still retained its autonomy and relinquished no authority to the new organization.

Nor did the fact that the two largest unions in the United States—the Teamsters and the Auto Workers—were now members of a single organization rather than of rival federations make any difference. Their economic value to each other was neither enhanced nor diminished by the merger. Interunion cooperation has never depended much on formal affiliations or formal ties. Indeed, unions have helped each other economically and financially for many years, generally without regard for the small niceties of affiliation. Consequently, such changes in affiliation as were wrought by the merger had little effect on interunion relations.

The merger also had very little immediate effect on the ability and power of unions to make gains in collective-bargaining negotiations, because the bargaining power of individual unions depends on economic conditions in their particular industry or occupation and, in the last analysis, on their ability to conduct an effective strike, rather than on the size of the federation of which they are a part.

Events since the Merger

The newly merged AFL-CIO shortly found itself faced with problems from an unexpected source—the Congressional investigations of corruption and misconduct in unions. The problems of corruption and racketeering in unions were by no means novel; they had plagued the labor movement at one time or another since 1900. What was unique about the problem in the mid-1950's was the extent of both public and official concern about it (particularly the latter).

To meet these problems, the AFL-CIO in 1956 and 1957 adopted a series of codes of ethical practices for union officials and backed them up with the power to suspend unions whose officers failed to adhere to them.

Expulsion of the Teamsters

By far the most dramatic application of these codes, of course, came in December 1957, with the suspension of the Teamsters Union for failure to oust its then president, the controversial James Hoffa. Today, perhaps the most lasting lesson to be gained from the Teamsters expulsion is its emphatic demonstration that the historic doctrine of the autonomy of national unions is a fact, not a theory. For when the AFL-CIO leadership, embarrassed and annoyed by the McClellan committee's findings about Hoffa,[23] wanted him out of office, they could only urge the Teamsters to remove him as president. The AFL-CIO was powerless to do so itself, for the Teamsters was (and is) an autonomous and independent decision-making body, and only the Teamsters Union had the authority to remove Hoffa.

When the Teamsters ignored its pleas, the AFL-CIO took the only step left to it—it threatened the Teamsters with expulsion unless Hoffa was removed. But this very act proved the AFL-CIO's lack of power to intervene; they could only impose the sanction of expulsion.

The result confirms this view. The Teamsters refused to oust Hoffa and were expelled from the AFL-CIO on a vote rather clearly split along craft and industrial union lines, with the industrial unions voting for expulsion, and the craft unions, particularly those in the building and construction trades—of which the Teamsters had been a long-time member—voting against it.

When the smoke had cleared, the AFL-CIO had lost 1.5 million members and some $900,000 in annual dues revenue and had failed in its objective of removing Hoffa. Their effort to dictate the Teamsters choice of officers had failed—they had been unable to overcome the real autonomy of the national union.

To add insult to injury, since the expulsion, despite all difficulties, the Teamsters has continued to grow—and at a pace faster than the AFL-CIO.

The Withdrawal of the Auto Workers

Ten years later, the AFL-CIO found itself faced with the loss of another major union, the Auto Workers. This time the issue involved differences between Walter Reuther, then president of the UAW, and the leadership of the AFL-CIO, especially George Meany, its president, over organizing, economic, and social policies, as well as rivalry between the two for the leadership of the Federation.[24]

[23]From 1957 through 1959, the McClellan Committee (the Select Committee on Improper Activities in the Labor or Management Field) held 270 days of hearings, and produced 58 volumes of testimony, over half of which dealt with racketeering and corruption in the Teamsters Union. See *infra*, p. 125.

After having served a prison term from 1967 to 1974 (although he remained as Teamster president until 1971), Hoffa's sentence was commuted by President Nixon. Hoffa disappeared in July 1975 and is believed to have been murdered.

[24]A. H. Raskin, a veteran observer of the labor movement, once asserted that "Reuther, frustrated at his own steady decline of influence within the federation and convinced that Mr. Meany would never quit, led his Auto Workers out of the merged movement." *The New York Times,* October 6, 1975, Section 4, p. 3.

In any case, the break began in February 1967 when Reuther resigned from the AFL-CIO Executive Council. It widened in May 1968 when the UAW was suspended for nonpayment of per capita taxes, and was completed in July 1968 when the Auto Workers withdrew from the Federation, taking with them some 1.4 million members. Although Reuther subsequently died in a plane accident in 1970, the UAW has remained independent and has shown no signs of returning to the Federation.

Kirkland Becomes AFL-CIO President

1979 marked a major change in the leadership of the AFL-CIO. At its convention in November, George Meany, who had been president of the Federation since the merger in 1955, and before that, president of the AFL from 1952 to 1955, stepped down and nominated Lane Kirkland, the Federation's secretary-treasurer, to succeed him. Meany died two months later, in January 1980, at the age of 85.

Kirkland thus became the fourth federation president since the founding of the AFL—preceded by Gompers, Green, and Meany. While it is obviously too early to predict how this change will affect the policies and the direction of the Federation, it is significant that in his acceptance speech, Kirkland said that "all true unions belong in the American Federation of Labor and Congress of Industrial Organizations"[25]—an open invitation to the reaffiliation of the Auto Workers and the Teamsters. Should they reaffiliate, it would increase the size of the federation by nearly 20 percent.

Kirkland also promised, on his second day in office, to explore ways and means to bring women and minorities onto the Executive Council. As we have seen, the election of Joyce Miller to the Council in August 1980 fulfilled the first part of that pledge.[26]

The Merger after Twenty-Five Years

Meany's retirement also marked the twenty-fourth anniversary of the merger of the AFL and the CIO in 1955. As this is written, in 1980, the merger is rounding out a quarter-century, and it is appropriate to see

---

[25] *Proceedings, AFL-CIO Convention,* 1979, p. 288.

[26] For a far-ranging examination of Kirkland's style and of the state of the union movement as he took over its leadership, see A. H. Raskin, "A Reporter at Large: After Meany," *The New Yorker,* August 25, 1980, pp. 36–76.

the extent to which it has met the goals it set for itself in 1955, including doubling of its membership and revising the Taft-Hartley Act.[27]

As we have seen, the merger did not stimulate lasting growth in the AFL-CIO, whose membership by BLS measurements, is down slightly from its 1955 level. And although the lack of growth of the AFL-CIO since the merger is attributable more to the loss of its two largest former affiliates, the Teamsters and the Auto Workers, than to the lack of growth of the unions remaining in the Federation, the fact is that with regard to the impact of the merger on the size of the labor movement, neither the hopes of the architects of the merger nor the fears of the business community have been realized.

And certainly the political record of the AFL-CIO since the merger suggests that it is not invincible. It *is* a major political force in the United States; perhaps even as George Meany claimed, "the single most effective political organization in the country"; but it is not an irresistible force able to reach its objective over all opposition.

Nowhere was this more clearly demonstrated than in the failure to win passage of the Labor Law Reform Act in June 1978, when a two-year legislative drive to put what organized labor regarded as essential new teeth in the Taft-Hartley Act was thwarted by a five-week-long filibuster in the Senate; efforts to obtain the 60 votes required for cloture fell short by two votes.

On the other hand, the AFL-CIO lobbied vigorously *for* the passage of the Civil Service Reform Act, which passed in 1978, and it participated in an intensive and successful campaign to defeat a "right-to-work" Constitutional amendment in Missouri in 1978.

On balance, the political record of the twenty-five years since the AFL-CIO merger is more or less a draw in terms of major labor legislation.

The Employee Associations

Just as the American Federation of Labor originally provided the model for organizing skilled workers, and the Congress of Industrial Organizations the model for organizing the semi-skilled, so the employee association may prove to be the model for organizing professional and white-collar employees who are willing to organize and to engage in collective bargaining, but have reservations about being identified with a union per se. In the ten years since the Bureau of Labor Statistics

---

[27]See Eugene H. Becker, "Meany Farewell, bid to Auto Workers, Teamsters mark AFL-CIO Convention," *Monthly Labor Review,* February 1980, p. 60. This report also includes a thoughtful assessment of the general results of the merger.

began to collect data on them, employee association membership has grown from 1.8 million to 2.6 million, a gain of 800,000, or 45 percent.

In 1978, over 90 percent of the membership of employee associations reporting to the Bureau of Labor Statistics were state and local government employees. Less than 2 percent were federal employees, and only 6 percent were employed outside the public sector, primarily in nonprofit hospitals, colleges, and universities.

At the same time, two-thirds of all employee association members were teachers—1.7 million in the National Education Association and 56 thousand in the American Association of University Professors. Another 187,000 members were nurses. All told, then, over two-thirds of employee association members were professional employees.

It should be emphasized that the employee association is not a new organizational form. What *is* new, however, is that many long-established employee associations have recently become involved for the first time in representing their members in collective bargaining—the key function of a labor organization—often in conjunction with their more traditional role of lobbying on behalf of their members.

Although employee associations have established themselves as a vital and growing segment of the American labor movement, their membership so far has been generally confined to government employees, with a heavy emphasis on teachers. Whether employee associations can expand significantly beyond their present limits to the professions generally, and whether they can compete successfully with unions, will determine whether they are truly a different model of organization and a solution to the general problem of organizing professional and white-collar workers.

Anatomy of the Labor Movement

The structure of the American labor movement—the interrelationship of its component parts—is as complex and intricate as its 24-million-member size suggests. Basically, this structure or organizational anatomy consists of two major parts: the labor unions, which for many years *were* the labor movement, and the employee associations, which have become a recognized part of the labor movement only within the past few years.

The organizational structure of the labor unions consists of three major segments or levels: the federation, the national unions, and the local unions, each with its own distinctive and special functions. Although they are separate and distinct from the unions, employee associations are comparable to national unions in function—and may have branches or chapters comparable to local unions.

The Federation

At the center of the American labor movement (not at the head, because it does not control) is a single major federation, the American Federation of Labor and Congress of Industrial Organizations, generally referred to simply as the AFL-CIO. The AFL-CIO, like the United Nations, is a voluntary association, and is composed of free and autonomous labor unions. Accordingly, a union may be an integral part of the American labor movement without joining the AFL-CIO. While the AFL-CIO is therefore not all-embracing, it does include the great majority of national unions. In 1978, 105 of the 173 national unions belonged to

43

the AFL-CIO. Their combined membership was 15,550,000, or slightly more than 70 percent of total American union membership.[1]

A further analogy between the AFL-CIO and the United Nations may be noted. Just as individual citizens do not become members of the United Nations, individual workers do not become members of the AFL-CIO, but join one of the national unions affiliated with it. If their union should leave the AFL-CIO for any reason, as did the Teamsters in 1957 and the Auto Workers in 1968, the individual workers' membership in their union is not changed, because they belong to the *union,* not the Federation.

The AFL-CIO is, in short, a union of unions, not of individuals. Membership in the Federation, in fact, is virtually confined to national unions. Although the Federation does include a scattering of locals that belong to it directly, rather than to a national union, their membership is scanty—only 27,000 in 1979, or less than two-tenths of 1 percent of total AFL-CIO membership—and their role is negligible.

Contrary to popular belief, the control of the 105 national unions affiliated with it is *not* centralized in the AFL-CIO, for it has long been a keystone of AFL (and now AFL-CIO) policy that in joining the Federation a national union does not surrender its independence or sovereignty. In the terminology of the labor movement, the national unions are autonomous organizations, essentially free agents, setting their own policies, making their own decisions, and retaining full control over their own affairs. It is the officials of the national unions who decide whether to strike and what demands to make in negotiations, not the officers of the AFL-CIO. It has been well put, in fact, that the Federation exists at the wish of the national unions, rather than the other way around. The Federation has neither the formal authority nor the effective power to dictate the behavior of its constituent unions.

The plain fact is that the AFL-CIO is not directly involved in the fundamental union function of collective bargaining. For all practical purposes that function is reserved for the national unions and, to a lesser extent, for the locals.

The primary role of the Federation, instead, may be described as broadly political. The AFL-CIO is to organized labor roughly what the United States Chamber of Commerce is to business; it is engaged in lobbying, public relations, research, and education to present labor's views on countless problems—not only on wages, hours, and working conditions, but also on topics ranging from public housing to foreign policy.

[1]From "Article by AFL-CIO President Kirkland on Union Membership, and Membership Statistics from Report Prepared by AFL-CIO," in *Daily Labor Report,* February 25, 1980, pp. E-1–E-7.

It is interesting to note that the AFL-CIO itself claimed a membership of only 13,621,000 in 1979, based on per capita tax payments, as compared with the BLS figure of 15,550,000 in 1978.

In addition, the Federation performs various necessary functions within the labor movement. It charters new international unions, tries to minimize friction between affiliated unions and settle the disputes which occasionally break out between them, maintains a staff of organizers, and provides research and legal assistance primarily for unions too small to afford their own research staffs.

National Unions

After the Federation come the 173 national unions which provide the basic framework of the American union movement. National unions are more easily identified than defined; well-known examples of national unions are the Teamsters, the Auto Workers, the Steelworkers, the Carpenters, and the United Mine Workers. The Bureau of Labor Statistics, in compiling its biennial *Directory of National Unions and Employee Associations,* lists as national unions those having collective bargaining agreements with different employers in more than one state, federal unions holding exclusive bargaining rights, and all national unions affiliated with the AFL-CIO.

These national unions range in size from the 1.9-million-member Teamsters, which is not only the largest union in the United States, but probably the largest union in the free world as well, to the venerable International Association of Siderographers, AFL-CIO, which by 1979 had declined from its peak strength of 100 to a scant 15 members (siderographers are steel-plate transferrers, a printing trade).

The great metamorphosis of the American union movement in the past forty-five years is reflected in the changes in size of the largest national unions. In 1933, just before the great expansion of union membership, the largest union (then the United Mine Workers) had slightly less than 300,000 members, and only six reported 100,000 members or more. Forty-five years later, in 1978, the largest union reported 1,924,000 members; five had a million or more members each; a total of fourteen had passed the half-million-member mark, and no less than forty-four claimed membership of 100,000 or more.[2]

With such disparities in the size of national unions, membership tends to be concentrated in the largest unions, just as business assets or sales tend to be concentrated in the largest corporations. Thus in 1978, the six largest unions accounted for 7,662,000 members, or 35.3 percent of total American union membership; and the ten largest for 10.4 million members and 47.9 percent of the total. These levels of concentration in

---

[2]In June 1979, the merger of the Retail Clerks and the Meat Cutters resulted in a new union, the United Food and Commercial Workers, with a total membership of 1,200,000 members.

the six largest and ten largest unions are not new, however, and in fact
are virtually the same as they were a half century ago.

Somewhat surprisingly, however, the largest union accounts for a
smaller share of total union membership now than during the first
quarter of this century. Thus the Teamsters' 1.9 million members represented only 8.9 percent of total union membership in 1978, as compared with the average of 11.2 percent represented by the United Mine
Workers during the forty-one years when *it* was the largest American
union. In 1978, in fact, it would have required over 3.8 million members,
or nearly double the Teamsters' actual strength, to match the record
share of 17.6 percent of total membership in the United Mine Workers
in 1901.[3]

While the evidence indicates unmistakably that the *concentration*
of union membership is neither new nor increasing, the rise of individual unions to such great absolute size has undoubtedly been one of
the prime factors in the development of the sentiment that union power
needs to be checked and controlled. As is discussed below, however,
size and power are not necessarily closely related.

If the Federation performs a basically political function, the 173
national unions (whether members of the AFL-CIO or not) are the chief
executives of the economic function—namely, collective bargaining.
And since the American labor movement is distinctive for its emphasis
on economic activities—a policy which goes back to Gompers—the
national union, by virtue of its collective bargaining function, has
emerged as the dominant force in the American labor movement.

To be sure, collective bargaining is not the sole prerogative of the
national unions, for there are many cases in which local unions still play
the decisive role in collective bargaining, chiefly in the building trades
or service trades, where product markets are essentially local in character. And even where the national union controls wage negotiations,
there remain distinctive local issues which assure the local unions a
significant bargaining function. But economic change and the broadening of product markets have tended to widen the area covered by a
single collective-bargaining agreement (since, as we shall see, unions
are forced toward applying uniform terms to all competitors) so that it
often extends beyond the scope of the local union and shifts into the
hands of the national union. As improved transportation and communications have hastened the growth of national markets at the expense
of the local market, the national union has gained power accordingly.

Each national union has its exclusive jurisdiction, or territory, in
which it claims the right to organize workers and control jobs. To use

[3]Marten S. Estey, "Trends in Concentration of Union Membership, 1897–1962," *Quarterly
Journal of Economics,* Vol. LXXX (August 1966), pp. 347–349.

a business analogy, a union's jurisdiction is comparable to an exclusive sales territory or franchise. No union is to compete for the workers in the jurisdiction of another, although, as the frequency of jurisdictional disputes indicates, they often do.

The jurisdiction of most national unions has been spelled out, at least initially, in the charter issued them by the AFL-CIO. (Of course, many charters long antedate the merger, having been issued by the AFL or the CIO.) But many unions have, on their own initiative, amended and modified the definition of their jurisdiction as the industries or occupations in which they operate have changed, or as their own objectives have widened.

Because in fact they represent something like a legal document, jurisdictional definitions are often extremely detailed, as for example that of the Teamsters Union, which claims jurisdiction over:

> all workers including, without limitation, teamsters, chauffeurs, warehousemen and helpers; all who are employed on or around horses, harness, carriages, automobiles, trucks, trailers and all other vehicles hauling, carrying, or conveying freight, merchandise, or materials; automobile sales, service and maintenance employees, garage workers and service station employees, warehousemen of all kinds employed in warehouse work, stockmen, shipping room employees, and loaders, that is, persons engaged in loading or unloading freight, merchandise, or other materials onto or from any type of vehicle; all classes of dairy employees, inside and outside, including salesmen; brewery and soft drink workers, workers employed in ice cream plants; all other workers employed in the manufacture, processing, sale and distribution of food, milk, dairy and other products; all truck terminal employees; and cannery workers.[4]

This broad jurisdiction has expanded from one basically limited as late as 1932 to local delivery drivers (of coal, ice, milk, and bread), until today the Teamsters is perhaps the closest American counterpart of the English *general* union, which in effect claims unlimited territory.

The aggressive imperialism of the Teamsters, in fact, has given rise to the joke (not entirely facetious) that "if it moves, it's a truck; if it has four walls, it's a warehouse."

And, indeed, the authoritative study, *Hoffa and the Teamsters,* makes it clear that from the outset of his activities in the union Hoffa's credo was to organize all the workers he could get his hands on and that in the 1930's and 1940's he often disregarded the traditional boundaries of Teamster jurisdiction; since then he had "explicitly rewritten the

---

[4]*Constitution* adopted by the Miami Beach, Florida, Convention, July 5–8, 1971. International Brotherhood of Teamsters, Chauffeurs, Warehousemen and Helpers of America. Article II, Section 1, p. 4.

[Teamsters'] International Constitution to eliminate such retarding limitations."[5]

In contrast to the practically limitless jurisdiction claimed by the
Teamsters, that of the Marine Engineers Beneficial Association includes:

> **All marine engineers who have been licensed by the Bureau of
> Marine Inspection, United States Coast Guard, to serve as such on vessels
> of the United States. Marine engineers regularly serving on commercial
> motor vessels operating in inland waters where license requirements
> have not been established by the Bureau of Marine Inspection in Nav-
> igation.[6]**

The difference in the breadth and scope of these jurisdictional
claims leads us to the fact that national and international unions can (in
a broad sense, at least) be classified, according to the nature of their
jurisdiction, as either craft or industrial unions. While these two categories, or structural types, can be expanded to six or seven,[7] the dis-
tinction between craft and industrial unions is a basic one.

Craft unions, of course, are those whose jurisdiction concerns a
particular skilled *occupation* or occupations. Thus, among the traditional craft unions we would find the Carpenters, the Plumbers, the
Bricklayers, and the Painters. Membership in such unions is a function
of being employed in a particular occupation, irrespective of industry.

Industrial unions, on the other hand, define their jurisdictions in
terms of particular industries or groups of industries, and membership
is a function of employment in the industry, regardless of skill or occupation. The best-known examples of industrial unionism, no doubt,
are the Auto Workers and the Steelworkers.

In practice, of course, there are many departures from, and exceptions to, these basic definitions. Industrial unions may not be all-inclu-
sive of employees in an industry—for example, an industrial union may
include only the production workers in an industry and make no attempt to organize its white-collar and office employees; or it may in fact
be multi-industrial (as the Auto Workers union is). Craft unions may
not, in fact, confine themselves to a single occupation, but go on to
embrace a group of related occupations.

It would be pointless here to attempt a complete classification of
union structural types; the essential point, as we shall see later, is that
the question of structure has been a major source of controversy within

---

[5]Ralph C. James and Estelle Dinerstein James, *Hoffa and the Teamsters: A Study of Union
Power* (Princeton, N.J.: D. Van Nostrand, 1965), pp. 81–82.
[6]*Handbook of Union Government Structure and Procedures: Studies in Personnel Policy*,
No. 150 (New York: National Industrial Conference Board, Inc., 1955), p. 23.
[7]Jack Barbash suggests that unions may be identified as "craft, multi-craft, trade, semi-indus-
trial, industrial, multi-industrial, and nondescript." See Jack Barbash, *The Practice of Unionism*
(New York: Harper & Row, 1956), p. 88.

the American labor movement; a union's structure directly affects its behavior, its policies and interests, and, in many cases, its long-run growth or decline.

Independent National Unions

Outside the AFL-CIO are what are generally referred to as the independent unions, which are the national unions not affiliated with the AFL-CIO.

The sixty-eight independent national unions active in 1978 had a combined strength of 6,200,000 members, or 28.5 percent of total American union membership. The reasons for their independence vary widely—the Brotherhood of Locomotive Engineers never joined a federation; the United Mine Workers has been independent since it withdrew from the AFL in 1947 in a policy dispute. The United Electrical Workers and the ILWU were expelled from the CIO in the late 1940's for alleged communist domination, and the Teamsters from the AFL-CIO in 1957 in a fight over union ethics and the presidency of Hoffa, and the Auto Workers withdrew in 1968 in another policy dispute.

Local Unions

The third level in the union structure is the local union. Local unions, as a rule, are branches of national unions, although a few are affiliated directly with the AFL-CIO or are completely independent. All told, there are now approximately 65,000 local unions, ranging from the 56,000-member Local 32-B of the Service Employees International Union, which represents building service employees in New York City and is larger than many national unions, down to locals having seven or eight members, the minimum required by national union constitutions to qualify for a local union charter.

The bulk of local unions, like membership, is concentrated in a few national unions. Some 22,000 local unions, or more than one-third of the total, are affiliated with six national unions having 2,000 or more locals each. And the fourteen national unions with 1,000 or more locals each accounted for over 34,000 locals, or more than half the total number reported in 1978.

The vast majority (over 98 percent) of local unions are subdivisions or chapters of one or another of the 173 national unions. But the relationships between a national union and its locals are much closer than between a national union and the Federation. Autonomy, such as that which the national union has *vis-a-vis* the Federation, does not exist for the local union. Local unions are not only chartered by the national union, but may be disbanded, suspended, or put under administration supervision (trusteeship) by the national union (subject to the terms of the Landrum-Griffin Act). Many union constitutions require local unions to obtain permission from the national union before calling a strike (or if not directly requiring it, make the payment of strike benefits contingent upon such clearance); representatives from the national union office may be sent to assist local unions in collective bargaining negotiations or in handling grievances. In short, local unions generally lack the unrestricted decision-making authority of the national unions.

Like their parent national unions, local unions may be broadly classified as craft or industrial unions. The scope of local unions also varies according to the size and nature of the community in which they operate. Locals of an industrial union may be specialized according to occupation or industry (the Teamsters' locals in major metropolitan areas tend to specialize according to industry) or by plant (as with the Auto Workers). In small towns, one craft local may cover the whole area.

Although much of its collective bargaining function, especially on economic issues, has been yielded to the national union, the local union has by no means been reduced to insignificance or impotence. Even in industries where the nature of the market requires national union control of general wage negotiations, local issues—problems unique to particular plants and localities—are of fundamental importance. The 134-day General Motors strike of 1970, in fact, was caused by local issues. Thus the *national* contract, covering wages, pensions, insurance, retirement and vacation benefits, was signed November 11, but the last dispute on *local* issues was not resolved until January 26, 1971.[8]

Even more important, the local union reaches the worker "where he's at." The local union is the individual member's point of direct contact with his or her union; its performance is the basis on which the worker judges not only the local but perhaps the national union and the labor movement as a whole.

And the local union is judged primarily on its handling of the grievance procedure, the process by which the collective bargaining agreement is administered and interpreted. It is the local-union officer, not the international representative or someone from the Federation, who gets the individual member's complaints about how he or she is treated in the plant. And it is the local-union officer who, in effect, is responsible for winning or losing the grievance for the worker. If the grievance is settled in favor of the worker, the local—and through it the national union and unions generally—looks good; and if the grievance is lost, unionism may suffer.

---

[8]U.S. Department of Labor, Bureau of Labor Statistics, "Collective Bargaining in the Motor Vehicle and Motor Vehicle Equipment Industry," (no date), pp. 1 and 2.

Similarly, active, interested, and effective local leadership tends to produce a favorable reaction from the members, and vice versa. In short, the local union *is* the union to the members. Its performance is the basis for their opinions of unions.

Independent Local Unions

Independent local unions are perhaps the most independent of all, for they are affiliated with neither the AFL-CIO, nor, like the majority of locals, a national union; their activities are generally confined to a single establishment, employer, or locality.

The 899 independent local unions responding to a Bureau of Labor Statistics survey in 1976 were estimated to have a combined membership of 331,559 in 1978.

Interunion Relationships
State and Local Central Bodies

The AFL-CIO has branches, or subordinate units, at both the state and local level, which it refers to as state and local central bodies. In June 1979, there were central bodies for fifty states and Puerto Rico, and 744 local central bodies.[9]

The function of both state and city central bodies closely parallels that of the AFL-CIO itself: their primary concerns are state and municipal legislation, political action, and community relations—in short, lobbying and public relations.

Like the main federation, these state and city central bodies are organizations of unions, not individuals. Local unions whose parent national unions are affiliated with the AFL-CIO are *eligible* for membership in their respective state or local central bodies (as are directly affiliated locals), but membership is neither automatic nor compulsory. As a result, less than 45 percent of the nearly 57,000 locals in AFL-CIO unions were members of their state and local central bodies in 1979.[10]

Departments and Councils

In addition to coordinating lobbying and public relations efforts through the vehicle of the state and city central bodies, unions frequently find it desirable or necessary to coordinate their economic

---

[9]*Report of the Executive Council of the AFL-CIO,* Thirteenth Constitutional Convention, Washington, D.C., November 15–20, 1979, p. 43.

[10]*Ibid.,* p. 51.

activities as well, particularly in situations in which a number of unions face common economic problems. Perhaps the best known of these groups for coordinating activities between national unions or between their local unions are the trade and industrial union departments and their local counterparts, the trades and industrial union councils—literally, councils of unions active in a particular industry or group of related trades. Perhaps the archetype of all trades councils is that of the building and construction trades councils. In these councils, and their national union counterpart, the Building and Construction Trades Department of the AFL-CIO, seventeen national unions (including, for example, the Carpenters, Electrical Workers, Bricklayers, Painters, and Plumbers) deal with the mutual problems which they face because all are active in the same industry. These problems are not always labor-management problems; some of the thorniest, in fact, are jurisdictional problems between one union and another. But there is no doubt as to the effectiveness of their united action against the employer, as any contractor will agree who has had *all* union workers on a job walk off because of his dispute with members of *one* union.

The device of the Building Trades Council, in fact, provides the craft unions with one of the advantages of industrial unionism without sacrificing the values of the craft union. As such, it has proved a most valuable mechanism.

In addition to the building trades department, the AFL-CIO provides special departments for the food and beverage trades (established in 1976), the maritime trades, the metal trades, and railroad employees, as well as an industrial union department, a public employee department (established in 1974), and a professional employee department (established in 1977).[11]

Other less formal relationships may be established for special purposes, such as coordinating negotiations with a common employer. The Industrial Union Department in 1979 was servicing approximately twenty-five coordinated bargaining committees, and some sixty-five more were in the formative stages. Another example is provided by joint organizing campaigns, such as the Los Angeles–Orange County campaign launched in 1963, with forty cooperating unions, which by 1979 had organized a total of 371,500 workers.[12]

Intraunion Ties

Unions that are closer in structure to the industrial union than to the craft union but whose locals are specialized either according to the products handled or by occupations within an industry require *intra-*

[11]*Ibid.*, pp. 332–365.
[12]*Ibid.*, p. 51.

union coordinating mechanisms. Thus, in many metropolitan areas there are what are known as *joint councils* or *joint boards*. Unlike the trades councils, which are composed of locals of different international unions, the joint councils consist of locals of a single national union, each with special problems distinct from the others, but all with the mutual bond of affiliation with the same union and the same basic industry. Typical are the Joint Boards of the International Ladies' Garment Workers and the Joint Councils of the Teamsters.

Thus, in New York City, the New York Joint Board of Coat, Suit and Allied Garment Workers Unions and Affiliates (formerly the New York Cloak Joint Board) includes four ILG locals: Local 1 (Coat and Suit Workers of Manhattan and the Bronx), 23–25 (Blouse, Skirt, and Sportswear Workers), 35 (Pressers) and 48 (Coat and Suit Workers of Brooklyn, Queens, and Staten Island).[13]

And 30 different locals, with a total of over 100,000 members, make up Philadelphia Teamsters Joint Council 53. Also, in the Teamsters, which is almost a "general" union, the advantages of sharing, on a national basis, common knowledge about special problems has been provided by the creation within this multi-industrial union of "trade divisions" and "trade conferences," such as the National Warehouse Division, the Bakery Conference, and the Brewery and Soft-Drink Division.

Similarly, many large unions are regionalized for administrative and executive purposes. But regionalization can serve more than administrative efficiency; the Western Conference of Teamsters, created in the early 1940's by Dave Beck (then simply the head of a Teamsters local union in Seattle), provided a political base for his election to the presidency of the Teamsters in 1952, just as Hoffa's control of the Central States Conference of Teamsters gave him control of the largest bloc of votes in the International Union and made him politically almost invulnerable.

Employee Associations

In 1978, the Bureau of Labor Statistics provided data on 26 professional and state public employee associations that engaged in collective bargaining and related activities. Together, they represented 2,561,000 members, or slightly more than 10 percent of the total U.S. membership of unions and associations.

Generally speaking, the organizational structure of the employee associations is simpler and less hierarchical than that of the labor unions. Although some thirty-three state public employee associations

---

[13]*Report of the General Executive Board of the International Ladies Garment Workers Union* to the 35th Convention, Miami Beach, May 31, 1974, pp. 123–125.

are affiliated with the Assembly of Governmental Employees, there is no central federation of employee associations comparable to the AFL-CIO.

The largest employee association is the National Education Association, with a reported membership in 1978 of 1,696,000, in 11,000 affiliates; the NEA is thus the second largest labor organization in the country, after the Teamsters.

Four other associations reported memberships of 100,000 or more in 1978—the American Nurses Association, 187,000; the Classified School Employees, 150,000; the Fraternal Order of Police, 140,000; and the California State Employees, 105,000.

At the other end of the scale, we find associations of professional athletes, such as the National Basketball Players Association, with 242 members in 22 clubs, or the Major League Umpires, with 48 members.

The Management of Unions

It is customary to describe the internal organizational structure of a labor union in political terms and to compare it with the organizational structure of a business firm, paying particular attention to the ultimate sources of authority in each case.

Although employee associations, as we have noted, have now entered the collective bargaining arena, and although they resemble labor unions in many respects, this chapter deals specifically with the management of unions.

The Power Structure

The organizational structure of the labor union is referred to as democratic, because its chief officers are *elected* either by the general membership of the union or by their delegates at national union conventions, rather than appointed by their predecessors or their fellow officials. Top union officers are therefore responsible and accountable to the membership and, in the last analysis, must satisfy them if they are to stay in office. The final authority therefore rests in the hands of the members, not the officers. In this case, power flows from the bottom of the organizational pyramid to the top.

In the business firm, on the other hand, final power and authority rests either with the owners or stockholders or with *appointed* officials to whom it has been delegated; power flows from the top down, and its organizational structure is described as *authoritarian*.

It should be emphasized that these labels are intended to be neither

55

critical nor complimentary, but simply descriptive of particular relationships between the upper and lower levels of a hierarchy. The fact that
the labels may seem complimentary or critical reflects the tendency of
Western societies to place a higher value on democratic than on authoritarian government or administration.

Structure alone, of course, is not the only determinant of an organization's political and administrative style. Union officials, no less than
other politicians, are adept at building political machines and utilizing
a democratic structure to their advantage. Thus, the reader may recall
flagrant examples of dictatorial union leadership (as well as impressive
illustrations of democratically run businesses), for it is quite true that
the character of an organization can be significantly affected by the way
in which it is administered. But that does not alter the basic point of the
analysis, which is that the *organizational structure* of one institution is
democratic while that of the other is authoritarian.

The elections through which the membership exercise their ultimate control of the union are generally held at local union meetings or
at the national union convention. In a relatively few cases, voting for
union officers is done by referendum or by mail ballot. The national
union convention is often both a legislative and a judicial body, providing
for a vote of the membership on dues and assessments, on constitutional
changes, and, in some cases, on appeals from executive decisions made
since the previous convention, as well as for election of officers.

But the election is a periodic event which, according to law (the
Landrum-Griffin Act), national unions must hold at least every five years.
In the interval between elections, therefore, the administration of the
national union is generally left in the hands of an executive council or
executive board, similar to the board of directors of a corporation. And
between executive-board meetings, the actual operations of the union
are carried out by the president and the executive officers, with the
assistance of various and sundry staffs, boards, and committees.

Quite aside from constititutional powers, the general president of
a national or international union is likely to wield great *de facto* powers.
This stems from the fact that, as some writers have put it, the president
is, in effect, the commander-in-chief of an army[1]—a fighting organization whose predetermined single objective is to advance the economic
interests of its members. In many cases, the president is the chief union
negotiator in bargaining with management, and in this capacity, controls
the key function of the union, guiding it through its most crucial mo-
ments. Here the president must make the command decisions, determining what action is necessary to meet the requirements of the situ-

---

[1]A. J. Muste, "Army and Town Meeting," in Bakke, Kerr, and Anrod, *Unions, Management, and the Public,* 3rd ed. (New York: Harcourt, Brace, and World, 1967), p. 168.

ation. Union policy, set by the convention or other means, can provide guidelines, and the collective bargaining decisions may require approval of the members, but the president is the chief executive, and like any other executive, must make decisions when they are called for.

Furthermore, having access to the facts and figures, and having had the opportunity personally to judge and interpret management's behavior at the bargaining table, the union president has the advantage in answering the critics and the doubters among the members and is generally able to convince the membership of the wisdom of the decisions made.

Ultimate Authority of the Membership

The ultimate authority of the rank and file is no mere textbook proposition, however, but an operational reality, as has been vividly demonstrated in recent years.

In a majority of unions, collective bargaining agreements negotiated by union officers and staff must be ratified by the membership before they become effective. Of course, ratification is often just a *pro forma* ritual, because, as we have suggested, union leaders politically astute enough to be elected to office are likely to be able to persuade the membership to accept their recommendations. But the formality must still be observed, and since the passage of the Landrum-Griffin Act, with its emphasis on union democracy, there has been an increasing tendency for the membership to reject proposed collective bargaining settlements as unsatisfactory and to send their leaders back to the bargaining table—for more.

Thus the Federal Mediation and Conciliation Service reported that in fiscal year 1978, "the rate of contracts rejected following an agreement between the parties neared the 12 percent point for the first time in twelve years,"[2] while the average for years 1969–1978 was 11.0 percent. This serves to emphasize the extent to which the membership *does* exercise final authority over the union's stand in collective bargaining.

And perhaps no year in recent union history gave more dramatic evidence than did 1965 of the fact that the rank and file is still able to exercise its power to determine who its officers shall be, and that even established leadership may be voted out of office. In that year, we witnessed the defeat of the incument presidents of the United Steelworkers

[2]Federal Mediation and Conciliation Service, *Annual Report,* 1978, p. 26.

of America, the third largest union in the country, and of the International Union of Electrical, Radio and Machine Workers, as well as those of several smaller national unions.

It would be unrealistic to regard these as simple manifestations of popular discontent, when instead they may be more appropriately described as palace revolutions—the outcome of power struggles at the top. But the fact remains that these changes have been carried out by the mechanism of a vote of the membership, and the factions fighting for control have had to conduct their contest in the open and wage their fight in the form of a fight for voter support—a true political contest.

Membership Participation and Apathy

But this evidence that the membership can and does play a vital role in union government should not be interpreted to mean that the well-known problem of membership apathy—the tendency of the rank-and-file member to let George do it and leave the decisions to the leaders—has been solved.

Whatever the reasons for this apathy—whether the issues are becoming so complex that they cannot be properly evaluated by the ordinary member; whether traditional union emphasis on economic objectives leaves the membership with the attitude that the union is simply providing an insurance function or a public-service function, which it is up to the administration to perform as best they can; whether the sheer size of the typical union today leaves the member feeling that his or her vote cannot change things anyhow; or whether the union meeting simply cannot compete for the member's spare time with the many recreational activities available—whatever the reasons, it is an observed fact that attendance at union meetings is usually confined to a small fraction of total membership. Only 10 or 15 percent of the members may turn out for an ordinary union meeting, and even such critical decisions as election of officers or the ratification of a proposed collective bargaining settlement may bring out a bare majority of members.

The agreement between the Transport Workers Unions and New York City's Metropolitan Transportation Authority, reached in April 1980 after an eleven-day bus and subway strike, was subsequently ratified when the membership, in a mail ballot, voted 16,718 to 5,417 in favor of acceptance. Although the vote was more than three to one in favor of agreement, the total vote cast represented only 70 percent of the 31,000 members involved.[3]

---

[3]*Government Employee Relations Report* No. 862, May 19, 1980, p. 34.

When it comes to turning out to vote in the election of union officers, still another factor must be borne in mind if we are to understand member behavior. The election process in American unions differs from the typical election for public office because the candidates, especially at the national union level, generally run unopposed. Unions typically do not have a two-party political system, with an incumbent party and a recognized and accepted opposition party. Only one national union, the Typographical Union, has a two-party political system.

Lacking a system which "legitimizes" opposition, incumbent officials are generally nominated to succeed themselves, and they generally face the final stage of election unopposed. Nomination, accordingly, is often equivalent to election. Offered no choice, and unlikely to benefit from rejection of the candidate at the last minute, the members' apathy and indifference to the outcome of the election under such circumstances seems inevitable. Even in the 1972 rerun election of the president of the United Mine Workers, one of the most highly publicized union elections in American history (because it followed the murder of the losing candidate in the original 1969 election), only about two-thirds of the members eligible to vote actually did so.

On the other hand, when the choice is whether or not they wish to be represented by a labor organization, workers are far from apathetic. Thus in NLRB representation elections in fiscal 1979, approximately 90 percent of those eligible did vote.[4] Indeed, it is consistent with the economic orientation of business unions that the response of the membership to decisions involving their union appears to be a function of the economic impact of the issue.

Thus, when strike authorization is sought from the membership, it is generally approved by a substantial margin. This consistent tendency to support the leadership on the strike issue is understandable, however, when it is realized that to reject a strike call is not simply a vote of no confidence in the leadership; more seriously, it amounts to a decision on the part of the members not to fight, a decision to send their leaders to the bargaining table not only unarmed, but conspicuously so, for management is publicly informed of this fact by the outcome of the vote. Thus, because it is contrary to the worker's self-interest to weaken his or her union's bargaining position, a vote to reject a strike is rare.

But to reject a contract settlement is quite a different matter. The members are likely to see this as simply a way of *improving* their position—for the effect of rejection is to send their leaders back for more. The risks seem negligible and the possibilities of improving their position appear good.

Similarly, the well-known resistance of members to dues-increase

[4]National Labor Relations Board, *Forty-fourth Annual Report,* 1979, p. 16.

proposals—perhaps the most difficult proposals to push through a union convention—arises from the adverse effect these increases, at least in the short-run, have on their pocketbooks.

To put membership apathy into historical perspective, it should be noted that this problem is neither recent nor a function of the growth of large unions, as one might suspect. Instead, we find the Webbs reporting complaints of union apathy in London as early as 1890:

> Only in the crisis of some great dispute do we find the branch meetings crowded, or the votes at all commensurate with the total number of members. At other times, the Trade Union appears to the bulk of its members either as a political organization whose dictates they are ready to obey at Parliamentary or other elections, or as a mere benefit club in the management of which they do not desire to take part.[5]

And to put the alleged apathy of union members into a current context, the fact is that union members take about as much part in their union—when major decisions are involved—as the citizens do in national political decisions. Thus in the 1972 presidential election of 140 million eligible voters only 78 million, or 55 percent exercised their right to vote—a slightly smaller proportion than voted in the 1972 Mine Workers election.

The point we wish to stress, in any case, is that high levels of participation, as measured by voting activity, are not typical of people either as union members or as citizens. People are as active in exercising the right to vote in their union as they are in national political affairs. And while we may feel that their union is of more immediate concern to union members, and that they *should* take more part in it, it is *their* union, not ours; they must decide how it is to be run.

The Union Managers

Those who run the union from day to day and set the course of action it is to take (subject to the veto of the membership), are its officers and staff, who may properly be considered the union managers. Indeed, lest we appear to be stretching a point to talk of managers in a union context, it should be noted that in at least one union, the International Ladies' Garment Workers, the chief executives of local unions are known as *managers*.

Understandably, the most distinctive (though by no means the most important) qualification for elected union officers is essentially political

---

[5]Sidney and Beatrice Webb, *The History of Trade Unionism*, rev. ed. (New York: Longmans, Green and Co., 1920), p. 465.

rather than managerial—they must have worked their way up from the ranks and spent some time in the trade or industry whose workers they represent.

Unlike corporate executives, whose managerial talents are readily transferable and who can move with relative ease from one industry to another, union leaders rarely, if ever, shift from one union to another, less because their managerial talents are too specialized than because rank-and-file attitudes still discourage it. The complete professionalization of union management has not yet taken place.

Salaries

The compensation of union officials has been a matter of considerable public interest, often critical of the levels to which it has risen.

Thus a 1980 *Business Week* survey of the salaries of the fifty-four top union leaders reported that "Eleven . . . either received over $100,-000 last year or received raises that will soon move them over that mark."[6] The highest salary reported was the $156,250 paid Teamster president Fitzsimmons, but the average salary plus allowance of those surveyed was a more modest $77,940.

In trying to appraise union officers' salaries, it quickly becomes apparent that there is no objective standard upon which they can be judged and no figure which can be reasonably established as to what union officers *ought* to be paid for their services. Should they be paid according to the size of their union? If so, the president of the Teamsters *should* receive the highest salary in the labor movement. But even if we accept that criterion, we are still faced with the question: What should the highest salary in the labor movement be? How can we justify a salary of $156,250 for the head of the Teamsters? Or, for that matter, why shouldn't it be more? We *might* look at what it costs the individual union member—with 1.9 million members, the cost per member is roughly eight *cents* per year, hardly a heavy burden and perhaps even a low price for vicarious adventure. No matter how we appraise the problem, there is no objective answer.[7]

Ironically enough, the same issue of *Business Week* puts the issue into sharp perspective with a survey of the compensation of 507 executives of twenty-five companies. The report identified twenty-five executives who earned more than $1 million in 1979, eight who received over $2 million, and one, the chief executive officer of MGM, who earned more than $5 million.[8]

[6]*Business Week*, May 12, 1980, pp. 86–89. The report refers to fifty-six union leaders, but gives data on only fifty-four.

[7]For an interesting discussion of this issue, see Leo Troy, "American Unions and Their Wealth," *Industrial Relations*, May 1975, Vol. 14, No. 2, p. 134.

[8]*Business Week, op. cit.*, pp. 56–57. These high incomes were primarily due to the exercise of stock options rather than to salaries.

Tenure

Closely related to the interest in union officials' salaries is the question of how long they do, and should, serve in office. Here again, it is the exceptional cases which attract attention. It is well known, for example, that the Teamsters Union was led by one man for forty-five years. Dan Tobin became president of that union in 1907,[9] when it had only 36,000 members, and continued in office until 1952, when it had over one million members. John L. Lewis assumed the presidency of the United Mine Workers in 1919 and remained for thirty-nine years, until 1958.

As is the case of officers' salaries, there is no standard as to the proper length of service for union officials any more than there is for corporate officers, many of whom hold their positions for comparable periods of time.

But because of the union's democratic structure and the union emphasis on its contribution to democracy in the workplace, the question can be raised, with somewhat more force and validity than in the corporate case, whether long tenure on the part of union officers is compatible with the democratic image the union claims for itself.

The evaluation of this problem involves both constitutional technicalities and economic factors. The constitutional technicality arises from the way in which union constitutions are worded. An analysis of 111 national union constitutions, applicable to 96 percent of all union members in 1957, found that although the maximum term for union presidents was five years, "no constitution limited the number of terms a president could serve."[10]

Union constitutions, accordingly, impose no effective barriers to long tenure. And beyond a certain point, length of service in a leadership position tends to become self-perpetuating, whether in a union, a business, or in the political arena. The cult of personality becomes increasingly evident, and, as time goes on, criticism of union policy tends to be regarded as criticism of the individual leaders and comes perilously close to disloyalty, as well as organizationally risky for the critic.

The problem of replacing top union officials is compounded by several factors—officers' reluctance to exchange their income, prestige, and power for virtual oblivion (a sentiment they share with leaders of many other organizations); the general lack of any effective system for training replacements; and the fact that the internal organization of the union is more likely to discourage and to punish leadership ambitions among the younger members than to encourage or reward them.

[9]*The International Teamster* (July 1966), p. 5.
[10]U.S. Department of Labor, Bureau of Labor Statistics, *Union Constitution Provisions: Election and Tenure of National and International Union Officers, 1958.* Bulletin No. 1239, Washington, D.C.: U.S. Government Printing Office, 1958, p. 20. By 1972, however, at least four small independent unions did impose such limits. See BLS *Directory,* 1973, p. 63.

Coping with this issue, in fact, was the focal point of the AFL-CIO convention in 1979, when the 84-year-old George Meany, who had been president of the Federation since the merger in 1955, stepped down and was succeeded by Lane Kirkland, age 57, who as secretary-treasurer of the Federation for ten years, had been groomed for the position.

In fact, the change in the top leadership of the AFL-CIO is far more extensive than this; as of September 1980, more than half the Executive Council (twenty of thirty-three members) had been elected or appointed since 1975.

And of course, there is another side to the problem of the length of service of top union officials. The business union, as we have seen, gives its top priority to effective performance—to delivering the goods and to reaching its members through their pocketbooks. Efficiency, not democracy, in its internal affairs is therefore the guiding factor in union government. And although it is inseparable from the self-interest of the officials concerned, a strong case can be made that, given the emphasis on efficient and effective union leadership, long service (up to a point, at least) of union officers works to the advantage of the members.

The essential point is simply that experience in office pays off in greater bargaining skill, a better grasp of the economics of the industry, and better understanding and judgment of the management representatives with whom they negotiate. If there were a direct and continuous correlation between length of service and bargaining competence, it would of course be an almost unanswerable argument for long tenure. Certainly, there is persuasive evidence that the Mine Workers benefited materially from the long service of John L. Lewis or that the rank-and-file teamster benefited economically from Hoffa's bargaining skills. At the national-union level, particularly, it seems likely that frequent turnover of top officials would generally be more detrimental than beneficial for the membership, although it would be more democratic. It takes time for union officers to learn to make the most efficient and effective use of their new responsibilities. When Arnold Miller, after defeating Tony Boyle for the presidency of the United Mine Workers in 1972, first led negotiations for a major contract in the coal industry in 1974, he had to deal with the fact that the miners "expected their new leadership to negotiate a big settlement with the Bituminous Coal Operators," and that the Mine Workers Bargaining Council rejected his first tentative agreement with the operators as too small, and forced him to negotiate a new and larger settlement.[11]

Despite the apparently unvarying tendency toward long service in office of international union presidents, we are presently in a period of unusually high turnover in the leadership of major unions as a result of

[11]*Monthly Labor Review*, January 1975, p. 11.

both hotly contested elections and the fact that many well-known labor leaders are retiring, either by choice or as a result of a slow but increasing trend on the part of the unions to adopt compulsory retirement standards.

Thus in the two years 1978 and 1979, there was a turnover in the presidency of forty national unions—six of which were unions with memberships over 100,000 each.

The Decision-Making Process in Unions

Political and sociological factors, as well as economic ones, have a great deal to do with *how* unions make collective bargaining decisions and with what those decisions are.

Because union officials are elected rather than appointed, they must, regardless of the effectiveness of the political machines they may develop and regardless of the extent of formal membership participation in union decision making, maintain the support of the rank and file, who can (and do, if they are dissatisfied) reject hard-won contract settlements or, as a last resort, vote their officials out of office or turn to other unions.

Maintaining rank-and-file support in an economically oriented institution such as the American business union is largely a matter of delivering "more, now," for this is what workers want—and this is the standard by which they judge the performance of their union leader.

But the crucial question for the union leader is: How *much* more is enough? This question, in fact, lies at the heart of union decision making in collective bargaining, for the generalization that unions seek "more" gives us only the direction in which unions are driving. How does the union leader or the union negotiator decide that one offer is acceptable and another—sometimes only cents an hour lower—is not? What are the criteria by which the union negotiator determines that it is politically safe to make an agreement with management?

Comparisons

One answer to this question is to be found in comparisons. Rank-and-file union members obviously cannot make a complex economic analysis of the "package" their union leaders deliver at contract time. But they can and do compare what their union gets for them with what other unions get for their members. And since union members, like anyone else, have a great desire to keep up with the Joneses, a satisfactory settlement, for them, is one which is as good as or better than the next person's—while one that is not is unsatisfactory. *This* is the standard by which they judge the performance of their union leaders; this is the criterion applied to their record.

For example, the steelworker may compare himself to the auto worker. If Douglas Fraser wins a seventy-five-cents-an-hour increase for the Auto Workers, this becomes the critical point for the Steelworkers' officers, who feel constrained to win seventy-five cents an hour, or more. A sixty-cent increase would be unacceptable, for it would be "not as good" as the Auto Workers' settlement. More to the point, for the Steelworkers' officers to settle for less than the Auto Workers' officers would imply (whether justified or not) that *they* were "not as good" as Fraser; it would be politically unsafe, if not necessarily disastrous. An increase of *more* than seventy-five cents, on the other hand, would be grounds for rejoicing—a political victory of real value.

Although comparisons may be most compelling when they involve industries closely related economically to the member's own, comparisons may be made regardless of economic differences between industries. Economic conditions in the steel industry may be substantially different from those in the auto industry, but the workers in the two industries, nevertheless, are likely to expect comparable increases (it should be emphasized that we are talking about comparable *increases*— not identical terms of employment in both industries).

It is obvious, of course, that the Steelworkers do not have to compare the collective bargaining achievements of their union leaders with those of the Auto Workers. They could compare them with the Mine Workers, or the Teamsters, or the Carpenters—in fact with the performance of any of the 173 national unions currently operating in the United States.

Here is where union leadership comes into play. Part of the union leaders' role is to influence the comparisons their members make. Indeed, the selection of suitable and advantageous comparisons is not only the way the leaders convince their membership a good job has been done, but it is an important aspect of collective bargaining, for the latter is essentially a matter of negotiating over *which* comparisons are right—the union making comparisons which justify its demands and the management negotiators pressing those which favor their position.

In any case, the union leaders' success in convincing the members of the validity of comparisons offered them may be instrumental in determining whether the agreement won is acceptable to them. Of course, once a particular set of comparisons is "sold" to the membership by the leaders, it tends to become the standard comparison. The union leaders, therefore, tend to operate within a fairly fixed set of comparisons. Because the leaders have "sold" them to their members in previous years, they know in advance just what comparisons the members are likely to make.

The Steelworkers compare with the Auto Workers, in the last analysis, because at some time past, the Steelworkers' officers made this comparison. But once having made it, the leaders are stuck with it. They know that the comparison will be made, so the Auto Workers' settlement becomes the minimum that the Steelworkers must get. Rather than accept less, they will strike.

The importance of comparisons as a determinant of wage demands has undoubtedly been enhanced by the growth of collective bargaining in the public sector, where a combination of limitations on the right to strike and the absence of profits as a guide to ability to pay lead to an even greater emphasis on comparisons than in the private sector.

Economic Factors

Economic factors do enter the picture, of course, sometimes through the comparisons we have been discussing. Economic conditions in an industry, especially as they are reflected in profits, are an important indicator to the union of management's ability to pay—one of the major determinants of union wage demands.

Thus one of the factors in the determined stand of the United Mine Workers in the bituminous coal strike in 1978 was the fact that high profits of the coal companies, and the likelihood that they would remain high because of the renewed importance of coal as a fuel, made an above-average settlement a political necessity for the union, whose top leadership, as we have seen, was new and untested.

Perhaps equally important in determining the size of wage demands, especially in the inflationary economy of the 1970's and 1980's, has been the rise in the cost of living (technically, the consumer price index). When wage increases fall behind price increases, as they did during much of 1978 and 1979, the amount of goods and services a worker's paycheck will buy—real wages—declines, and the pressure to correct this situation at the next negotiation becomes irresistible. To avoid this, many contracts now provide for automatic cost-of-living adjustments in wages; in 1980, some 5.4 million workers were known to be covered by such provisions in union agreements.

Response to Membership Pressure

The 1980 New York transit strike also points up the very real dilemma of the union leader involved in a strike in a crucial industry. The public is bound to be highly critical of the inconvenience, hardship, and economic loss resulting from the strike and is likely to assume that the problem is basically a matter of stubbornness and indifference to the public welfare on the part of the union leader. What the public generally fails to realize is the extent to which the union leaders' obduracy in such situations is the result of pressure from their membership—the result of their insistence that the leaders hold out for more. Seldom has this point been more forcefully demonstrated than during the 1966 airline strike when a tentative settlement, negotiated under White House auspices and announced by President Johnson himself, was rejected by the membership by a margin of more than two to one.[12]

And while there is a constant expectation on the part of the public that in this situation union leaders will yield on their demands and be "responsible" to the public interest, this expectation completely ignores the fact that the union leaders' first responsibility is to their members. This is not merely a matter of loyalty, it is a matter of the most direct self-interest, for it is the members, not the public, who will decide whether the union leaders keep their jobs.

Ironically enough, the sensitivity of union leaders to rank-and-file pressures has probably been increased by the Landrum-Griffin Act— more, perhaps, by its general focus on the rights of the members than on any specific provision—whose passage may in part be attributed to vigorous pressure from employer groups.[13] But having seen the effects of greater union democracy (not the least of which may be higher costs to them), employers are showing signs of wishing for a return to one-man rule in unions—to "responsible" union leaders with final authority to make a binding decision which management can be confident will not be rejected by the membership. Thus, for both management and the public, it is evident that union democracy in the form of membership power to veto collective bargaining decisions is not an unmixed blessing.

The role of comparison in union decision making sheds light on another point that is widely misunderstood. Unions do not really push in each negotiation for "all they can get." Dramatic though it sounds, the fact is that unions want to leave something for next time. Even more to the point, union leaders generally are interested in getting only enough to satisfy their membership; to fight for more than that is simply a waste of time and energy.

Of course there are occasions and situations in which a union leader wants to outdo other leaders by as wide a margin as possible. But generally, union leaders want to live to fight another day; they want to have something to get next year and the year after. Politically, if

[12]*The New York Times,* August 1, 1966.
[13]Doris B. McLaughlin and Anita L. W. Schoemaker, *The Landrum-Griffin Act and Union Democracy,* Ann Arbor: The University of Michigan Press, 1979, p. 179.

they meet the standard of comparison or exceed it somewhat, they are safe.

If it takes hard bargaining to win a fifty-cent package, it is harder to win a fifty-five or sixty-cent package. If, in the judgment of union negotiators, fifty cents is politically safe, they are not likely to push for fifty-five or sixty cents—because, in economic terms, they are as interested as the next person in achieving their goal (in this case, membership approval) at the lowest possible cost. The union leader may misjudge the membership sentiment, as we have seen, but membership rejection of proposed contracts is illustrative of a corollary of the point we have just made. It is the rank and file, contrary to popular opinion, that are often the most aggressive and demanding, rather than the leadership. It is more often a case of the rank and file being the militants and the leadership trying to restrain them, than of the leaders dragging unwilling members out on strike against their wishes or insisting on holding out for gains unsought by the members.

And there is a reason for this. Leaders not only tend to grow away from the rank and file as time goes on (and the problem is doubtless aggravated in the larger unions), but they also become, through repeated dealings with management, inevitably more aware of the complexities of the problems over which they are bargaining and more aware of the substance of management's position. No sell-out to management is required for the union leaders to become, as time goes on, more conservative than their members in the interpretation of what can be obtained.

Bargaining Within the Union

The decisions confronting union officers concern not only how much to demand from management, but also how much is enough to satisfy the membership. Equally important is what the package is to consist of—how the gains won from management are to be distributed. A fifty-cent package can take a number of forms and vary in a number of ways: in terms of its division between direct wage increases and fringe benefits; in terms of how the direct wage increase is distributed as between, say, skilled and unskilled workers; and so on, almost *ad infinitum.*

The distribution of these gains is no minor matter; it is of crucial importance to the internal politics of the union. The union is not only an agent for the negotiation and settlement of the conflicting interests of management and labor, but it is equally a mechanism for resolving and balancing the conflicting interests among its members.

George Taylor expressed it concisely when he said that one of the main functions of a union is "to discern, reconcile, and then represent the diverse and often conflicting demands and interests of its memberhip."[14]

One such problem of reconciling conflicting needs within its own membership is that confronting the United Auto Workers. As is typical of an industrial union, the great bulk of the UAW's membership falls into the semi-skilled category. Political necessity therefore dictates that the collective bargaining program of the union and the distribution of collective bargaining gains reflect this fact. At the same time, however, there is a small but important group of highly skilled workers—die-makers, model makers, etc.—whose economic leverage as a group cannot be overlooked. So the union periodically has to negotiate special or supplementary benefits for the skilled workers to compensate for the fact that the regular negotiations tend to be tailored to fit the needs of the semi-skilled majority. Thus, in the 1973 negotiations with Ford, the skilled workers' rejection of the settlement forced the revision of overtime provisions to which they had objected.[15]

One advantage of the craft-union type of organization, in terms of decision making, is that, because of the essential similarity of the problems that members face, the community of interests of the members is relatively great and conflicts of interest relatively small. In the industrial union, on the other hand, the variety of jobs held by the membership inevitably produces a variety of interests among them, many of them unavoidably conflicting. The leadership of the craft union, accordingly, is probably called upon to devote less of its time to resolving *internal* differences of interest among its members than is the leadership of the industrial union; craft-union administration appears to be less complex than that of the industrial union.

The experience of the United Auto Workers affords another example of the problems of balancing different needs within a union. The General Motors strike of 1970, which closed assembly plants for 134 days immediately after the 1971 models had been introduced in September, is generally conceded to have occurred, not because either the leaders or the membership were dissatisfied with the general economic gains offered by the company, but because the rank and file felt that in the course of several successive contract negotiations "local issues" had been subordinated to national ones. While the problem undoubtedly represented the focus of a number of factors, it is nonetheless believed that Woodcock felt impelled to permit a strike to resolve such local problems as washroom time and smoking privileges because they had become too important to the members to set aside any longer.

[14]George W. Taylor, "The Role of Unions in a Democratic Society," in *Government Regulation of Internal Union Affairs Affecting the Rights of Members*. Selected Readings prepared for the Subcommittee on Labor and Public Welfare, United States Senate, by the Legislative Reference Service, Library of Congress (Washington, D.C.: U.S. Government Printing Office, 1958), p. 19.
[15]*Monthly Labor Review,* January 1974, p. 77.

And a strong case can be made for the view that in spite of his undeniably effective overall collective bargaining record as president of the Steelworkers Union, David McDonald's loss to I. W. Abel by a narrow margin was due to the way those gains were distributed. The evidence indicates that McDonald actually led Abel by a slight margin among Steelworkers in the United States and that the 10,000-vote margin by which Abel won was just about the size of the *Canadian* membership of the union, which allegedly voted against McDonald because they felt that during his thirteen years in office he had consistently discriminated against them in the distribution of collective bargaining gains. Whether their belief was justified is less important than the fact that the experience demonstrates how crucial *internal* bargaining can be.

Centralization of Decision Making: The Shift of Power to the National Unions

Another important aspect of union decision making is the long-run trend toward centralization of power and authority in the national unions, primarily in the form of increased control of collective bargaining decision making and execution. This centralization of union decision making is due not to any single factor, but to the combined effect of a number of factors.

One of the key factors responsible for this continuing shift of power from the local to the national union is an economic one—the growth of a national market for products. Because this is so fundamental to an understanding of how unions operate, let us look at the problem in detail.

In competitive industries, the presence of nonunion firms is a barrier to further gains for union members and a threat to the security and survival of the union. Accordingly, out of sheer economic necessity, unions tend to expand toward their economic limit—the organization of all firms competing in a particular market, whether it is a product market or a service market. And having organized them, the union must then push to eliminate wage differentials among them in order to take wages out of competition.

Given these economic pressures to expand to the limits of the competitive market, it is obvious that anything which affects the extent of that market, anything which affects the area of competition, will affect the extent of union activities.

What has happened and is continuing to happen is that the extent of the market is changing—the area of competition is becoming broader and broader. As our transportation system and our communications have improved, product markets have spread, so that today the majority of products compete and are sold in regional or national markets rather than in local markets, as was formerly the case.

The broadening of the product markets, however, means more than just a further expansion of union organizing objectives or a further expansion of the number of firms subject to a single collective agreement. Sooner or later, the expansion of the product market extends the area of competition beyond the jurisdiction of the single local union. It brings firms in one locality into competition with firms in other localities. And when this happens, the economic terms of the collective agreements made by local unions in one community become immediately relevant to locals active in the same industry but in other localities.

To put it another way, when the product market has extended beyond the boundaries of the single community, bringing two or more communities into a single competitive area, the union is faced with a repetition of its original problem—it still needs to "take wages out of competition." But now the problem changes; it is no longer simply a matter of wage differentials between union and nonunion firms. When several different locals of the same national union are making collective bargaining agreements on wages and all are operating within a single competitive area, the existence of differentials between one *union* wage level and another creates the same problem as the wage differential between union and nonunion firms—low union rates are a drag on the further advancement of higher ones. The solution to the problem of differential wage settlements made by locals within a single competitive area is coordination—ensuring that all locals within the area of competition apply uniform terms so that there are no differentials and none of the problems that differentials create.

While there are many ways in which local-union bargaining can be coordinated (in fact, some of the structures noted in Chapter 3 owe their existence to the need for such coordination), perhaps the most common solution is simply for the national union to take control of the negotiation process. This is what has happened: the extension of the product markets has created a situation in which coordination of collective bargaining patterns of different local unions is required, and this has led, increasingly, to the assumption of control over collective bargaining by the national unions.

In those industries in which the product market has remained predominantly a local one, the local union tends to remain in control of collective bargaining, more or less independent of the national union. But in industries whose product market is national in scope, the responsibility for collective bargaining over economic issues (although, because of the veto power of the membership and the pressures involved in internal bargaining, not always the *control* of it) has tended to shift to the national union, leaving the local union with primary responsibility for bargaining over local issues and for day-to-day administration of the contract.[16]

It is intriguing to speculate whether the combination of trends toward greater democracy within unions and a revival of interest in noneconomic issues (which may be relatively neglected in national bargaining) might also have modified the distribution of power within the labor movement, shifting it away from the national and toward the local union.

The building trades and the auto industry provide practical illustration of the differences between industries in which the local union still controls collective bargaining and those in which control is held by the national union.

Decision making in the building trades is decentralized not because of some stubborn determination by local union officials to resist the loss of control to the national union, but because the product market of the building trades remains (and seems likely to remain) predominantly local in character. Buyers of housing are not likely to pull up stakes and move lock, stock, and barrel to buy a house in another city simply because housing is cheaper there. The fact is, they want housing in their present community. And because the consumers are essentially unable to respond to *price* differentials between cities, the union, in turn, has no need to fear an adverse impact from *wage* differentials between cities. Builders in one city are not in competition (for these purposes) with those in another. Accordingly, local unions have pretty much retained control of the collective bargaining process, making literally hundreds of separate agreements, most of which are limited to a particular local market.

It should be noted, however, that in an effort to prevent inflationary pressures from upsetting and distorting established wage differentials and relationships, national union officers gained veto power over local union agreements, through their participation in the Construction Industry Stabilization Committee, established in March 1971. And even though CISC was disbanded in 1974, it may have permanently altered local-national union relations in the industry.

The auto industry, on the other hand, operates in a national product market. This, of course, is because automobiles, unlike houses, are shipped from the point of assembly to the retail market. And while assembly plants are located in many cities, the fact that the product is

---

[16]For an authoritative discussion of the role of the local union, see Leonard Sayles and George Strauss, *The Local Union* (New York: Harcourt, Brace and World, 1967).

shipped long distances to its final market means that the competitive impact of wage differentials would reach and carry adverse effects as far as automobiles can be economically shipped.

Were each local to negotiate independently and without reference to what other locals are doing, it would clearly pay the manufacturer to concentrate production in those plants where labor costs were lowest, so they could produce a given car at the lowest cost. But this would be detrimental to the employment and wage prospects of workers in the high-wage plants. In this case, then, the national union is compelled by economic factors to provide coordination between the decisions of different locals—in the form of national control and negotiation of master agreements applicable to all locals, regardless of where they are. And this is why wage guidelines could, if necessary, be applied with some degree of effectiveness in the auto industry—because in the auto industry collective bargaining decisions are highly centralized, so that the government's pressure could be concentrated at a single point.

The increasing shift of collective bargaining on economic issues from the local union to the national union is also stimulated by factors other than the pressure to prevent the corrosive effects of wage competition between locals.

Political or sociological factors may be equally important, for, regardless of the economics involved, workers think it only fair that an employer follow the policy of equal pay for equal work. So when a single employer has plants in different cities, the workers in each doing similar work, the pressure for *internal* consistency affects not only the employer but the union as well. If a number of local unions are involved, the necessity for coordinating their negotiations with a *single* employer becomes another factor pushing control toward the national union.

In the automobile industry, for example, the Auto Workers negotiate with General Motors, Ford, Chrysler, and American Motors one at a time, rather than simultaneously. But in 1979, the General Motors negotiations alone affected 460,000 workers, in 147 local bargaining units in 130 plants.[17]

Obviously, consistent treatment of members at General Motors requires a high degree of coordination between the many local unions involved (among other devices for accomplishing this is the National General Motors Council, which consists of representatives of UAW locals at these 130 plants); it has been achieved by national-union intervention and control of bargaining with the corporation.

Where a company's decision making is centralized and basic policy decisions (such as collective bargaining decisions) are not delegated to plant managers, the local union is confronted with management rep-

[17]*The New York Times,* September 9, 1979.

resentatives who have no authority to decide on their demands and who have to pass these demands on to "headquarters" for a decision. Accordingly, local union officers turn to *their* headquarters—the national union—so that those with the same degree of authority on both sides of the table can do the actual negotiations.

Still another factor pushing power and control into the hands of the national union is that of the growing complexity of collective bargaining problems. This has led unions, like their business counterparts, to make increasing use of staff specialists—economists, lawyers, accountants, etc.—to prepare the materials for collective bargaining. The sheer expense of maintaining such staffs is beyond the resources of most local unions; the expense of negotiating with big business is so great that only national unions can afford it.

This complex of factors—economic, sociological, administrative— then, has tended in the past to push an ever-increasing share of the collective bargaining process into the hands of the national union. And since collective bargaining is the central activity of the American business unions, it is customary to say that the national union is the backbone of the American labor movement—the basic member of the structure.

Today, however, the rapid growth of the service industries, whose markets are predominantly local and whose business organizations are more often medium to small in size, suggests that the trend to centralization of the collective bargaining function in the national unions may be ending and that, as union growth is increasingly concentrated in the service industries, local unions may play an increasingly important role in the bargaining process.

Meeting Institutional Needs

In the course of the extensive scrutiny to which unions and their internal activities have been subjected since the end of World War II, it has often been alleged that the union is not exclusively devoted to protecting and promoting the welfare of its members, but that some of its energies and resources are spent on its own behalf, as an institution to further the goals of the organization, as distinct from those of its members.

There is no question that this is a valid comment. The point is, however, that the union, like any other institution, is interested in its own survival and development. And indeed it must be, for it can hardly serve the interests of the members, either well or poorly, if it goes out of existence. So institutional survival and the pursuit of institutional goals are not in themselves inimical to the interests of the membership; in fact, they are essential for the welfare of the members.

Like so many of those involving union administration and internal government, the questions here are whether the share of union resources devoted to the welfare of the organization rather than that of the members is *excessive,* and whether, in any case, the methods or procedures used by the union in its self-interest are "good" or "bad."

Admission Policy

Compulsory Membership

One such institutional goal of unions is the so-called union security issue, or the question of compulsory union membership. Strictly speaking, what is involved are efforts by unions to make union membership a condition of employment—compulsory for those who want the job in a unionized plant. While anyone who is opposed to it can avoid the requirement by simply not working in a shop or plant where union membership is a condition of employment, union membership can be *virtually* compulsory, because the worker cannot find equally good work elsewhere. This point is very relevant, as we shall see later.

The union security issue is hardly new, for it was a part of the Philadelphia Cordwainers case in 1806. Most recently, however, it has been the basis of the fight over the right-to-work laws and the repeal of Section 14(b) of the Taft-Hartley Act, which is the legal footing of these laws. It should be made clear at the outset that the term "right-to-work" has nothing to do with a guarantee of employment, as it seems to imply, but is simply a euphemism for the direct prohibition of compulsory union membership.

In the last analysis, of course, the numerous arguments concerning compulsory union membership may be viewed simply as rationales of the real issue, which is simply the power struggle between labor and management. In this view, managements fight against compulsory unionism because they are opposed to union growth and increased power, which they see as a threat, no longer to their survival—or to the American way of life—but to their freedom to manage as they see fit. Unions fight for it, not only because it greatly simplifies their organizing efforts but because they believe, as management does, that it is an avenue to their growth and power.

The argument and the debate may not be entirely wasted, however, for it is designed among other things to influence public opinion and to tilt legislation in favor of one view or the other. There are two basic arguments in the fight over compulsory unionism: one, the union's argument; the other, management's. The basic union justification of compulsory unionism is the "free rider" argument, which stems from the fact that the Wagner Act and the Taft-Hartley Act make the union which wins a representation election in a plant the representative of *all* the workers in the bargaining unit, members and nonmembers alike. (Furthermore, these laws prohibit employers from discrimination in the terms of employment between union members and nonunion workers.) Consequently, in plants where the union bargains with the employer but lacks a compulsory membership requirement nonunion employees *must* get the same wages and fringe benefits that union members do, to comply with the law. The nonunion workers thus get the benefits of unionism without paying its costs (fees and dues); they are "free-riders."

Under these circumstances, of course, the union argues that since the law requires that *all* workers in the bargaining unit get its benefits, it is only fair that *all* should share in the costs—by being required to belong to the union. The union slogan might well be a switch on that of the Boston Tea Party: "No representation without taxation."

The chief management argument against compulsory unionism (and it is a *management* argument more than a nonunion *worker* argument) is that it interferes with the worker's freedom to choose whether he or she wants to belong to a union; that it is undemocratic and dangerous for a private organization such as a union to be allowed to force a worker to join in order to hold a job. Certainly this seems plausible enough; it is an argument designed to appeal to the true liberal, the defender of individualism. But there is a flaw in this argument, for the truth is that an essential ingredient of the effective functioning of the modern business organization is *standardization*—and not the least of the factors to be standardized are the terms of employment.

It is not an arbitrary management but the industrial process itself which dictates that employees start to work at specified times and that their work schedules be uniform. The point is, then, that generally speaking, individual employees have no choice as to the terms of employment in a particular plant. They cannot pick and choose the days they work, the hours they work, or the wages they will get; if they did, the result would be chaos. They take what is offered, or leave it. Economic necessity can make the terms of employment compulsory, whether the firm is unionized or not. And making union membership one of the terms of employment simply adds another requirement to those already imposed by the facts of industrial life. It *is* an additional restriction on the worker's freedom of choice, no doubt about it. But removing *that* restriction will not restore the worker's freedom of choice. It will not leave the worker free to choose his terms of employment; it simply means *one less* restriction to his freedom.

Indeed, it may be argued, without being too sophisticated, that the worker who is a member of a union at least has a voice in the demands the union makes on the employer and at least *some* voice in determining the terms of his or her employment. While the increase in the freedom of choice workers get in this manner cannot be quantitatively weighed against the freedom they lose by being required to join the union, it does seem that one tends to offset the other.

But there is a point at which the freedom issue is valid. There is a *conflict* of freedoms involved—the conflict between the freedom of the union members to work in a shop without nonunion workers and the freedom of the nonunion worker to remain nonunion.

Where there is such a conflict of freedoms, an accepted way to settle the issue, since there is no objective way to settle it on its merits, is to submit it to a vote and allow the principle of "majority rule" to provide the answer. This was done in the case of the union shop elections between 1947 and 1951, when a majority of workers involved voted in favor of the union shop.[18]

More recently, the issue of compulsory unionism was put to a vote on a broader scale when right-to-work laws were submitted to the voters in a number of states. In terms of practical politics, the outcome of these votes has been perhaps less a matter of the persuasiveness of arguments than of the composition of the population. In states with a large industrial and urban population, a large proportion of workers are union members who vote against right-to-work proposals because they regard them as attempts to weaken organizations which they find beneficial. And generally speaking, their votes have proved decisive.

This point was convincingly demonstrated in 1958, when, in six states—California, Colorado, Idaho, Kansas, Ohio, and Washington— right-to-work proposals were on the ballot. In the predominantly industrial states of California, Ohio, and Washington, as well as in Colorado, the proposals were defeated. Only in two agricultural states, Kansas and Idaho, did a majority vote for them. And more recently, in 1978, a referendum on a right-to-work constitutional amendment in Missouri, which includes the large metropolitan areas of Kansas City and St. Louis, was defeated by a margin of 3 to 1.

The result is that the nineteen right-to-work states are the predominately agricultural and rural states, in which the industrial worker is a minority and the unions are relatively weak.

Restrictions on Membership

Having been criticized for years for infringing upon the workers' freedom *not to join* a union if they choose (by their insistence upon making union membership a condition of employment), unions, perhaps ironically, have been criticized, especially in the last decade, for their tendency to restrict admission to membership, thereby infringing upon the

[18]See pp. 89–90.

worker's freedom *to join* a union if he or she chooses. Specifically, attention has recently been focused on the fact that many unions have pursued either formal or *de facto* policies of discrimination against blacks.

Restrictive membership policies, in fact, have a long history in the American labor movement. The skilled-crafts unions in particular have taken pains to restrict entry to their trades in order to limit competition for jobs and to maintain or raise the price of their members' services.

Viewed *solely* in these terms, restrictive admission policies are simply another facet of business unionism, one which reflects a shrewd grasp of the advantages businessmen have found in creating barriers to entry in their industries.

But viewed in the context of our prevailing concern for civil rights, such behavior, at least if it involves racial discrimination, is no longer acceptable—it violates both public policy (the Civil Rights Act of 1964) and public spirit. In *this* conflict of freedoms, the freedom of the individual to admission to a union on a nondiscriminatory basis takes priority over the freedom of union members to choose their colleagues.

A variety of devices has been used to limit and restrict membership. The simplest and most extreme was the closed union, which refused to admit anyone, usually because of declining employment in its occupation. And unions which ordinarily follow less restrictive policies may temporarily close their books to new members when regular members are unemployed.

Closely akin to closed unions were those which admitted only relatives of members. The Stagehands Union in New York City, for example, was ordered by the State Supreme Court in 1966 to admit three men who charged that although they had been working on a permit-card basis, they had been denied full membership because of union nepotism.[19]

Another device for limiting entry to the trade has been apprentice regulations, which are intended, among other things, to ensure proper training of craftsmen. But the apprentice program may become a device for discriminatory admission practices, for a worker who is not admitted to apprenticeship is not likely to become a union member.

None of these policies is *specifically* discriminatory, as between one group of applicants and another. But unions have discriminated, and do specifically discriminate, against women, Communists, Fascists, and subversives, and, most importantly, against blacks.

Racially discriminatory admission policies have included constitutional barriers by national unions, such as those of the Brotherhood of

[19]*The New York Times*, July 20, 1966.

Locomotive Engineers, which (until its 1966 convention voted to eliminate them in compliance with a court order) provided that no one could become a member "unless he is a white man" and required that applicants be sponsored by three members—a ritual allegedly used to bar nonwhite applicants.[20] The chartering of separate segregated local unions for blacks and other nonwhites has also been common, especially in the South.

Such constitutional and administrative barriers in national unions are now rare; indeed, those of the Locomotive Engineers may have been the last formal racial barriers in any national union constitution. But the problem of discrimination at the local level has been harder to eliminate. In particular, authoritative opinion suggests that efforts to end racial discrimination in the building-trades unions will remain difficult because of local autonomy in the building trades, nepotism as a basis for acquiring union membership, the economic power of the building-trades unions, and the traditional belief in the need to preserve limited job opportunities for a limited membership.[21]

Industrial unions, in contrast to craft unions, have generally found their interests more effectively served by an inclusive rather than a restrictive membership policy. Since, in the union shop, which is the common union security provision among industrial unions, the employer hires whom he pleases, the union goal is for *all* new employees to become members, for it is control of numbers rather than of a hard-to-replace skill that gives the industrial union its bargaining power.

Furthermore, it would be self-defeating for industrial unions to pursue a discriminatory admissions policy, for, as Slichter, Healy, and Livernash point out: ". . . in industries where a large number of Negroes, Puerto Ricans, Mexicans, or Orientals are employed, the industrial unions must take an aggressive stand against discrimination or give up the prospect of organizing the nonwhites."[22] As a consequence, the industrial unions have long been leaders in the drive to eliminate discrimination in employment and in union membership.

With the passage of the Civil Rights Act of 1964, of course, unions are prohibited from excluding individuals from membership because of race, color, religion, sex, or national origin; from segregating their membership on such bases; and from discriminatory practices in connection with apprenticeship programs. The public policy is clear; it only remains to be enforced.

---

[20]*Ibid.*, July 15, 1966.
[21]Ray Marshall, "Equal Employment Opportunities: Problems and Prospects," *Proceedings* IRRA Spring Meeting, 1965, p. 467.
[22]Sumner H. Slichter, James J. Healy, and E. Robert Livernash, *The Impact of Collective Bargaining on Management* (Washington, D.C.: The Brookings Institution, 1960), p. 53.

Fees and Dues

If what unions *pay* their officers is at one end of the financial spectrum, what unions *cost* their members is at the other.

The money costs of union membership are of two types. First and most important are those which affect all members, i.e., initiation fees and periodic dues (including occasional special assessments for one purpose or another). Second are those designed to meet special situations or problems and which affect only a small minority of members— transfer fees and work permits.

Recent data suggest that in 1974, union dues averaged about $10 per month per member, or about 1 percent of the average union member's annual income.[23] This ratio appears to be a fairly constant one, since it coincides roughly with our own estimate that in 1960, dues payments cost the union member, in real terms, less than two hours of work a month.[24]

Generally speaking, the level of dues (and of initiation fees as well) is related to the earnings in the occupation. Skilled-craft unions tend to have higher fees than industrial unions composed chiefly of semi-skilled workers. And high dues may also include premiums for special purposes such as death benefits and retirement, disability, and unemployment benefits.[25]

Although union dues may seem modest enough when judged by such standards, proposals to raise dues are likely to encounter opposition. Indeed, the first substantive issue with which Lane Kirkland had to deal, as newly elected president of the AFL-CIO, was the question of an increase in the per capita tax paid by affiliated unions to the Federation, and the opposition to it by, among others, the Musicians Union.[26] The increase passed handily, but the issue is symptomatic.

Initiation fees run somewhat higher than dues, in part because they are a one-shot charge, rather than a recurring one, and in part because they may be used to limit membership in a union and thus assist it in maintaining control of a particular labor market. On the other hand, it is not unusual for unions to waive initiation fees as inducement to join, especially for low-income groups.

Financial reports indicate that in 1974, although twenty-nine national unions reported initiation fees of $100 or more—usually organizations of specialized professions or crafts—the majority charged less than $40.[27]

[23]Charles W. Hickman, "Labor Organization's Fees and Dues," *Monthly Labor Review,* May 1977, pp. 19–24.
[24]Based on data from *Report of the Bureau of Labor-Management Reports, 1960,* pp. 26–27.
[25]Philip Taft, *The Structure and Government of Labor Unions* (Cambridge: Harvard University Press, 1954), p. 68.
[26]*Proceedings,* AFL-CIO Convention, 1979, pp. 296–302.
[27]Hickman, *op. cit.*

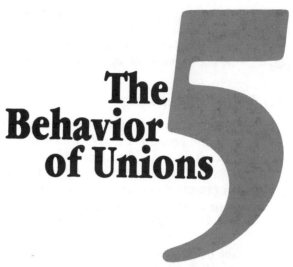

The Behavior of Unions

The mainstream of the American labor movement consists of what are generally referred to as *business unions*. Traditionally, the term business union has been used to distinguish unions whose goals are primarily economic from those whose objectives are primarily political or ideological. Business unions are chiefly concerned with what they call "bread and butter" issues—with winning better economic conditions for their members in the form of higher wages and fringe benefits, shorter hours, and better working conditions—rather than with what they have derisively called the "pie in the sky" objectives (long-run, "ultimate" goals) of the socialists and communists.

The purpose and objective of business unions may be summed up in the two words, "More, now." As Samuel Gompers, first president of the American Federation of Labor, testified before a Congressional committee in 1914, "...the best possible conditions obtainable for the workers is the aim," and when these conditions are obtained, "why, then, we want better...today and tomorrow and tomorrow—and tomorrow's tomorrow."[1] That description is as accurate today as it was then.

Market Orientation of Unions

But perhaps more to the point is that today's business unions are primarily market oriented; they concentrate on improving the terms under which their members *sell* their services. While it is true that they are

---

[1]See Leon Litwack, *The American Labor Movement* (Englewood Cliffs, N.J.: Prentice-Hall, 1962), pp. 40–41.

concerned with a wide variety of problems and issues which affect the worker away from the job (from education to housing to foreign policy), they focus the bulk of their resources and energies on one major target, the improvement of the conditions of their members at work.

Collective Bargaining

Unions accomplish this objective, in general, by negotiating directly with the employers who *buy* their members' services, rather than by placing primary reliance on government intervention and legislation. This process of negotiation between a union and the management of an organization over the terms of employment is known as collective bargaining. And so far as business unions are concerned, unions and collective bargaining are two sides of the same coin—inseparable.

Collective bargaining is thus a way of setting the price of labor in the market. But it is more than that. Collective bargaining is *the process by which unions share in making management decisions;* not all management decisions, to be sure, but those decisions involving the terms of employment and the price of labor. It would be a mistake to assume that unions are simply advisory bodies that suggest to employers what their members would like and let it go at that. On the contrary, once management has recognized the union as the representative of its employees, it has, perhaps unwittingly, but nonetheless effectively, yielded its right to make unilateral decisions with regard to the terms of employment and conditions of work in favor of sharing them with the union. By means of collective bargaining the unions become one of the institutions through which the business of management is conducted. *This* is the real significance of business unionism.

The impact of collective bargaining is not exclusively economic, however. It is also a major contribution to democracy in industry, for it provides the industrial worker with a mechanism for participating in making the rules under which he or she works.

Collective bargaining introduces democratic processes into the administration of business, government, and nonprofit organizations in a number of ways. It establishes a system of checks and balances against the arbitrary exercise of management authority. It brings with it not only a new way of *making* rules, as we have shown, but also a new way of day-to-day *interpretation* of the rules, known as the grievance procedure. The grievance procedure, which may properly be considered a continuation of the collective bargaining process, is essentially a judicial process, an appeals machinery to ensure that the law of the plant, as represented by the collective bargaining agrement, is properly applied and interpreted. The decisions reached through the grievance procedure become part of the common law of the plant, as it were.

And when the grievance procedure terminates in provision for voluntary arbitration, as is the case in nearly 90 percent of all labor-management agreements today, union and management of their own accord agree to submit unresolved disputes over interpretation of the contract to an outside party for binding decision, so that collective bargaining provides a peaceful but effective substitute for settling disputes by economic force.

Paradoxically, in any discussion of the impact of unions, it is easier to get agreement on the proposition that unions, through collective bargaining, have made a significant improvement in the lot of the employees by giving them a voice in the government of their industrial life than it is to win agreement on the *economic* consequences of unions and on the question of whether or not unions have raised wages above what they would otherwise be.

Though the discovery of the full implications of collective bargaining is often disconcerting to the employer engaged in negotiating with a union for the first time, collective bargaining has profoundly important benefits for management as well. For by *sharing* the decision-making function with management, the American union has developed into an institution designed to compromise with employers and to reach agreements with them, not to get rid of them. The basic objective of the American labor movement is not to eliminate the capitalistic system, but to share in its benefits. To be sure, unions are unhesitatingly eager to win a *larger* share of those benefits, but this is quite different from wanting to replace the mechanism which provides them. Labor does not seek to kill the goose that lays the golden eggs; it wants it to lay more golden eggs, and wants more eggs for itself. Though the extravagance of their bargaining demands often obscures it, business unions are properly described as conservative—staunch defenders of the existing economic system.

Unions which are most vigorous in pressing the employers in their industry for economic gains may be just as aggressive in joining with them to protect or promote the welfare of the industry as a whole.

The most notable recent example of such behavior, of course, is the role of the Auto Workers in trying to help the auto industry cope with the crisis brought on by the cumulative impact of rising gasoline prices, Japanese competition, and high interest rates, which in 1980 had brought the sales of domestic auto manufacturers to their lowest levels in twenty years, and brought the Chrysler Corporation, in particular, to the verge of bankruptcy.

In these circumstances, the UAW joined industry representatives in seeking import quotas to protect the domestic manufacturers from Japanese competition—a fairly traditional reaction.

But the Auto Workers' assistance to the Chrysler Corporation was without precedent in the annals of American business or labor. In what has already become a landmark in labor-management-government relations, it was the UAW's intervention that made possible the federal government's $1.5 billion loan guarantees designed to forestall Chrysler's bankruptcy. As one long-time observer put it, " . . . the Chrysler situation has distinctive elements unduplicated in industry generally. The most obvious is the extent to which the corporation's survival depends on the union. The virtually unanimous judgment in Washington is that Federal money would never have been forthcoming if the UAW had not mustered all of organized labor's lobbying power to push for favorable action."[2]

It should be emphasized that the Auto Workers' assistance was not confined to lobbying, important as that may have been. Its most important contribution was its willingness to make concessions of its own, in the form of postponing or yielding contract gains negotiated in September 1979, to help save the company. Initial concessions from the GM-Ford settlement patterns were valued at $203 million, and further concessions of $243 million were made at Washington's insistence.[3]

In return, the UAW won what is perhaps the most controversial part of the arrangement—a seat on the Chrysler board of directors for UAW president Douglas Fraser. Whether this marks the beginning of a new trend or is truly *sui generis* remains to be seen, as does the response of both union and corporate officials to Fraser's actions as a board member. And whether it is an essentially conservative move, to shore up and maintain an ailing corporation, or a leftward move toward European-style co-determination, is grounds for long and vigorous debate.

Such dramatic crises as Chrysler's, fortunately, are not common. But they do give added force to the traditional question of how long unions can continue getting "more, now" without encroaching on profits and interfering with business incentive. The question *is* a crucial one and should not be dismissed lightly. The saving factor here has been the long-run expansion of the economy and the rising productivity, which has raised real per capita income about 800 to 900 percent in the last century. So long as this sort of economic growth prevails, *both* labor and business (and indeed, all sectors of the economy) can have "more, now" year in and year out (with due allowance for economic fluctuations). So long as the economic pie is expanding, everyone can have a larger piece simultaneously.

But if the economy were to cease growing and stagnate, we would find ourselves in the situation in which one group could gain only

[2]A. H. Raskin, "The Labor Leader as Company Director," *The New York Times,* April 27, 1980, Section F, pp. 1, 14–15.
[3]*Current Wage Developments,* January 1980, U.S. Department of Labor, Bureau of Labor Statistics, p. 1.

at the expense of another—labor at the expense of business, or vice versa—and we would be in trouble. And it is precisely this prospect of intensified social and economic conflict over a very slow-growing—or even shrinking—economic pie that is raised by the dismal productivity record of the past few years, and by higher and higher world oil prices.

And if that situation were to materialize to a significant degree, we could expect more frequent and prolonged labor disputes, and more frequent resort to their economic weapons by labor organizations.

Here, too, their market orientation and their constant participation in the business world has made American unions remarkably business-*like* in a variety of ways. The weapons used by unions to press their demands in collective bargaining are chiefly market oriented. The strike, the boycott, and the picket line, for example, are all market mechanisms designed to put varying degrees of pressure on the employer by cutting him off from one or another of his markets. The strike interferes with the employer's access to the labor market; the boycott, with access to the consumer market; and the picket line, in addition to supplementing both the strike and the boycott, also impedes the employer's access to the product market.

Relations with Other Unions

Relations between unions are also noticeably market oriented. Like entrepreneurs who prefer monopoly for themselves and competition among their suppliers, unions are anxious to minimize the pressures of competition to control and limit it wherever possible. As we have seen, the practice of granting each national or international union its own exclusive jurisdiction, or exclusive franchise, was designed to provide it with a monopoly over a particular occupational or industrial territory, free from competition from other unions. In fact, no more devastating charge could be made against a union than that of "dual unionism" or "rival unionism"—of competing with another union in its territory, in which it regards both workers *and* jobs as its property. Nor is this view surprising, for many charters identify both the workers and the kinds of jobs over which the union is given jurisdiction.

Problems frequently arise, however, out of the definitions of the work over which a union has jurisdiction. Many of these definitions were written many years ago and drawn to describe industrial practices of the early twentieth century. As technology has changed and industrial practices with it, what were originally distinct and separate jurisdictions now are blurred or overlapping or rendered ambiguous by changing processes and techniques.

One well-known jurisdictional dispute brought about by just such circumstances involved the Carpenters and the Sheet Metal Workers.

Originally, the Carpenters' jurisdictional assignment gave them control over the installation of window sash, presumably because it was made of wood, the basic criterion of whether work belonged to the Carpenters. Sheet Metal Workers, on the other hand, claimed all work having to do with sheet metal. So far, no problem. But when metal window sash was introduced, the two unions found themselves in conflict; the carpenters claiming that metal sash belonged to them because *window sash* per se was carpenter's work, while the sheet metal workers claimed it on grounds that it was now made of the *material* with which they had the exclusive right to work.

We might expect at this point that two unions, for whom collective bargaining is literally a way of life, would find a workable compromise on this problem easy to arrive at. After all, as the contractor or builder who finds himself helpless in the middle of this dispute sees it, a little reasonableness and common sense on both sides would solve the problem; if both sides give a little, everything can be taken care of.

Instead, the ensuing disputes often rivaled in intensity the bitterest labor-management conflicts. For from the viewpoint of the Carpenters and of the Sheet Metal Workers, giving a little is no more sensible or reasonable a solution than for a manager to yield a little market to a competitor. Instead, they see the issue as setting a precedent, possibly countrywide, and not for today, but for an indefinite time in the future. If the Carpenters concede metal sash to the Sheet Metal Workers on one construction site, they may lose only a few jobs for carpenters, but multiply that a hundred times and the problem may look serious. And Carpenters Union officials are no more anxious than Churchill was to preside over the liquidation of an empire. Union officials, like members, are conscious of the scarcity of jobs; they do not cede control over *their* jobs readily. And from the Sheet Metal Workers' point of view, the problem is equally important—to fail to take advantage of expanding opportunities is to risk stagnation; it seems essential, as part of the unions' responsibility to the membership, to seize any job opportunities that come along. So what appears to the casual onlooker to be a petty argument often appears to the parties involved to be matters not merely of principle, but of institutional survival.

Disputes as to which union has the right to organize particular workers can be equally troublesome. The Retail Clerks and the Meat Cutters fought off and on for over half a century before their merger rendered moot the question of their respective rights to organize grocery clerks (or its counterpart, which jobs are "clerk's work"), and it was not uncommon to find the Clerks and the Meat Cutters competing for membership among grocery clerks in National Labor Relations Board elections.

Unions are not only opposed to competition among themselves

over members, which they regard, with some reason, as diverting energies from the main objective of improving the conditions of work; they are equally opposed to competition among workers for jobs, fearing that this kind of competition merely tends to drive down wages and aggravate an already unsatisfactory situation. Thus, it has long been a fundamental objective of union wage policy to "take wages out of competition"—to standardize wages as a means of preventing competition for jobs from driving them down. And the historic practice of limiting membership, most common in the old-line craft unions, was, whatever else may be said about it, basically a device to reduce competiton for jobs and thus maintain, or raise, the price of skilled labor.

Union Finances

The business-like character of unions carries over from their behavior in the labor market into their institutional life as well. Thus, collectively, and in some cases individually, labor unions are, financially speaking, substantial organizations. As would be expected of any institution with a total of over 21 million members, large amounts of money flow in and out of union treasuries, and substantial investments are built up over the years.

A survey of the financial status of unions based on reports filed in compliance with the Landrum-Griffin Act shows that the total assets of American unions (including those of locals, intermediate bodies, and national unions) amounted to $4.1 billion in 1977, while receipts and expenditures of local unions alone were in excess of $2 billion each.[4]

Impressive as these figures are in the aggregate, however, they show that union assets average roughly $200 per member. Or to put it another way, total union assets of $4.1 billion in 1977 would have ranked only 36th in *Fortune's* list of the 500 largest industrial corporations.

And while it is popular to focus on the financial status of the unions' giants—the Auto Workers in 1976 had receipts of $1.2 billion and assets of $233 million[5]—only half of all national unions had annual receipts of $1 million in 1976, and over half of all local unions had receipts of under $10,000 each.[6]

Ironically, some of the practices for which business unions and their leaders are most widely criticized stem from the business ethos. The high salaries and substantial expense accounts of some top union offi-

[4]*Statistical Abstract of the United States, 1979,* p. 428. For an analysis of union assets in 1969, see Leo Troy, "American Unions and Their Wealth," *Industrial Relations,* Vol. 14, No. 2, May 1975, pp. 134–141.

[5]*Union Financial Statistics, 1976,* U.S. Department of Labor, Labor-Management Services Administration, pp. 35, 37.

[6]*Ibid.,* p. 18.

cers, the lavish union headquarters which rival those of any business corporation, the union conventions in Miami and San Juan, the business agent's Cadillac—all this conspicuous consumption may be seen, in one perspective at least, as part of the union leaders' desire to emulate the employers with whom they deal, a desire to appear on equal terms with their counterparts across the bargaining table. And if occasionally union officials misinterpret what is acceptable business conduct, what could be more flattering than to be chosen as the model of behavior, the standard for the pattern of success? In part, too, this conspicuous consumption may be the logical result of the very philosophy of business unionism, for what is it but the epitome of "more, now"?

Generally speaking, such conspicuous consumption by union leaders, far from stirring resentment or envy among the rank and file, seems to give them vicarious satisfaction; they tend to identify with their leaders and to feel that generous spending by their union is indicative of its success. They seem to say, "Look what I can afford."

Besides, the typical union members, as we shall see, are mainly interested in what the union can do for them economically. Accordingly, they tend to judge their union and their union leaders by their own pocketbook. As long as their union is effective at delivering the goods, in the form of improved economic conditions, they are apt to be tolerant of its behavior in other aspects. Jimmy Hoffa's re-election to the presidency of the Teamsters Union in July 1966 (with an increase in salary from \$75,000 to \$100,000 a year), despite the prospects that before his term of office was over he might be jailed for jury tampering, should not be attributed simply to the effectiveness of Hoffa's skillful management of machine politics within the union, nor to a sporting insistence on the part of the members on sticking by a man when he's in trouble, although both factors were undoubtedly involved. Most observers would agree that Hoffa could have won a bona fide secret-ballot election hands down, simply because the membership had made substantial economic gains during his term as Teamster president.

There are limits to the member's tolerance, however, and the closer union leaders get to understanding and imitating the employers with whom they deal, the greater the risk they run of losing contact with their membership—a problem already grown acute in the largest unions.

The defeat of David McDonald in his 1965 bid for re-election as president of the Steelworkers, the third largest union in the country, is a pointed reminder of this fact. For, ironically enough, McDonald had more than met the traditional requirements of union leadership, economic gains of the Steelworkers during his thirteen years in office having been substantial. A frequently mentioned contributing factor in his defeat, however, was his maintenance of a residence in Palm Springs and his habit of spending long periods there, hobnobbing with Holly-wood stars and leaving the running of the union in the hands of his staff. Just how important this was will never be known, but in the bitter election campaign, the picture of McDonald in his tuxedo touring the night spots of Southern California was effectively used to portray him as a man who could no longer understand the problems of the man in front of the open hearth. The problem of communication seems en-demic to large organizations, regardless of their nature.

Why Workers Join Unions

When we begin to examine why workers join or fail to join unions, we find, of course, that there is not one reason, but a variety of reasons involved in their decision.

Compulsory Unionism

Today, of course, we must recognize that a substantial number of workers join unions because the firm or industry where they want to work is a *union shop* where, by union and management agreement, all employees must join the union if they want to keep their jobs. The *closed shop,* in which workers had to belong to the union in order to be hired, is no longer legal. In 1978, almost 90 percent of workers in contracts covering 1,000 or more workers each were subject to some form of union shop provision. The significance of this reason for union membership cannot be overlooked.

We should be careful, however, not to assume that in the absence of the compulsory-membership requirement these workers would have necessarily refrained from joining voluntarily. Some evidence of the fact that many workers would continue to join even in the absence of union-shop provisions is afforded by the experience in one of the nineteen states which, since 1947, have prohibited union-shop agreements—the so-called right to work states. In Texas, according to Frederic Meyers, unionization began to grow rapidly in 1938 and continued to do so with "no significant diminution"[7] when that state's right-to-work law was passed in 1947.

Compulsory unionism, in fact, may be much less repugnant to the workers subject to it than it is to the public at large. In this connection, a significant experience occurred during the period 1947 to 1951, when

---

[7]Frederic Meyers, "Effects of 'Right-to-Work' Laws: A Study of the Texas Act," *Industrial and Labor Relations Review* (October 1955), p. 78.

the Taft-Hartley Act required that, before a union-shop provision could be incorporated in a union-management agreement, it must be submitted to a secret-ballot vote and receive the support of a majority of those *eligible* to vote (as opposed to the customary requirement of a majority of those *voting*). Under this now defunct provision, not only was the union shop supported in 97 percent of all these elections, but, of over 5 million workers voting in them, nearly 80 percent voted in favor.[8] These overwhelming majorities in favor of the union shop, in fact, led Senator Taft, one of the sponsors of the Taft-Hartley Act, to urge successfully the dropping of the union-shop election provision on the grounds that the record indicated that it was a waste of the government's time and effort to put the question to a vote. As it now stands, therefore, the question whether the union shop is to become a part of a labor-management agreement is simply a matter of bargaining between the representatives of the parties.

Voluntary Unionism

Since neither the union shop nor the closed shop is possible until a union has been formed, has been recognized by an employer, and has negotiated a contract, let us return to the basic questions of why workers join voluntarily and why they form unions in the first place. Many theories have been advanced to explain workers' decisions when they are free to choose whether or not to join a union. The basic element in that decision can be stated quite simply: workers will choose to join a union if and when they think it pays off in terms of economic welfare or their status among friends and associates. The problem, therefore, is to distinguish the types of workers or the circumstances which fit these requirements.

The Unskilled

It is often supposed that the first workers to turn to unions as a solution to their problems were those who were economically the most depressed and exploited and whose working conditions most obviously called for improvement—namely, the unskilled workers. Such conditions may well have generated a strong *motivation* toward joining unions, but if so, such motivation was not sufficient. Successful unionization requires *both* motivation and economic leverage or bargaining power. Because the unskilled were readily replaceable, strikes or threats of strikes were probably more risky for the workers than for their employers. In short, their decision to quit or strike caused little hardship for their employers; they had no bargaining power—and unions without

8Benjamin J. Taylor and Fred Witney, *Labor Relations Law,* 2nd ed. (Englewood Cliffs, N.J.: Prentice-Hall, 1975), p. 329.

bargaining power do not pay off. Consequently, it has only been most recently, under special and unusual circumstances, that unskilled workers have been able to unionize successfully.

The Skilled

Thus, the first workers to unionize, in the United States as well as in Britain, were not the most downtrodden or the lowest paid. Far from it; unions first appeared among the economic elite of the working class, those whose wages were the highest and working conditions the best— the skilled workers, who had *both* motivation for organizing *and* the leverage to make the organization effective.

The skilled workers' initial motivation for organizing was originally less a desire to win "More, now" than a desire to protect the superior (for that period) economic position they already possessed from being undermined by competition from cheap labor. It is not accidental that many of the early unions called themselves "protective associations."

The competition which threatened the skilled workers took a variety of forms. In some cases, it was the arrival of new waves of immigrants, adding to the labor supply, with the predictable economic consequence that their availability tended to drive down the price of labor—that is, wages. And it was not simply that employers were willing to substitute new unskilled labor for their skilled employees, for the immigrants included skilled labor as well as unskilled. But the immigrants were often ignorant of local market conditions and, being used to the generally lower wages of countries from which they had come, were willing to work for wages lower than prevailed here. In such a case, those already employed might be confronted with the choice of taking wage cuts or being replaced.

More often, however, the competition came from lower-priced products made by lower-paid workers and sold in the market in competition with the products made by the skilled workers. Under these conditions, employers found that, unless they met the price of competing products, sales would drop and employment, too; this in turn led them to seek to cut labor costs as a way of preserving profits in the face of price competition. And again, high-wage employees faced the threat of loss of employment due to low-wage competition unless they could secure a uniform wage standard among all competitors.

Equally important was the fact that their skill gave these workers bargaining power. Unlike the unskilled worker, who could be quickly replaced, the craftsmen of the early eighteenth century could impose a real hardship on employers by striking. Their period of apprentice training was a long one, and the supply of workers in any skilled craft was relatively small. Accordingly, they were hard to replace, particularly if numbers of them ceased work simultaneously. And rather than face the consequences of trying to find replacements, employers frequently found it preferable to accede to the demands of the skilled workers and their organizations.

Unions first appeared among skilled workers, then, when these workers were motivated to protect their position and because their market position gave them the bargaining power necessary to make unions pay off effectively.

Undoubtedly the best known description of the *general* circumstances under which unions would meet the economic and social needs of workers is that of the late Professor Perlman of the University of Wisconsin.[9] His theory is that the American worker turned to unions only when he had concluded that he was not going to "get ahead" by moving up into the managerial ranks or by becoming self-employed. So long as he seriously entertained such hopes, joining a union was not the answer to his objectives, but was a tacit admission that he had abandoned them, an open recognition that he had given up the American dream of poor boy makes good. But whenever the worker recognized that the odds were heavily weighted against his getting a higher pay-off in this way, it became logical to turn to methods which would maximize the economic gains to be had *as employee*—in short, to join a union.

On the other hand, to those who look forward to moving into the managerial or supervisory ranks (white-collar workers, for example), or who expect to become self-employed, the probable pay-off from their individual advancement is likely to be greater than that offered by union membership.

Even the current labor organization among such professional groups as teachers, nurses, and doctors (see Chapter 1), though it does not match the *details* of this theory, is consistent with its *basic* point—namely, that the decision to join or not to join a union or an employee association is, among other things, an economic one.

Similarly, those who work part-time, or expect to be employed only a short time, such as young women who expect a job to be a rather brief interlude between school and marriage, are likely to see little economic reason for joining a union; the costs loom large, and the anticipated benefits to be gained in the course of short-run or part-time employment seem small. In these circumstances, their attitude tends to be: "I'm not going to be here long. Why should I join?"

Status

Another variable in the equation is status. It has often been argued that the demonstrated reluctance of many white-collar and professional employees to join unions is due to a fear of losing status, and to a feeling

[9]Selig Perlman, *A Theory of the Labor Movement* (New York: Macmillan, 1928), p. 321.

that unions are for blue-collar workers only. Thus a number of employee associations, whose members are typically white-collar and/or professional employees, have expressed "philosophical objections" to being identified as unions. Since this attitude has persisted long after the average weekly earnings of blue-collar workers moved above those of nonsupervisory white-collar workers, we must conclude that white-collar workers are willing to make economic sacrifices to maintain their status.

Perhaps what is really behind the status factor is the problem of conformity. Most of us, whether at home or at work, tend to conform and find it easier and more comfortable to follow the practices and behavior of the majority. For this very reason, both union strength and union weakness tend to be self-reinforcing.

If a union has already achieved success in a community, is well established, numerically strong, and accepted, the new employee is likely to see membership as part of the prevailing pattern and to join, if only to do as the Romans do. If the union includes only a small minority, as is still the case for most white-collar unions, membership tags one as part of that minority; thus, belonging is nonconforming behavior, and the typical reaction is to avoid it. The union problem in this case, of course, is how to make the transition from minority to majority status.

In light of this analysis, it is most significant that a recent survey of how American workers view labor unions revealed that "workers generally viewed unions as large, powerful bodies, which are highly effective," and perhaps because of this, "of the nonunion workers [responding to the survey] almost one-third said they would vote to unionize."[10] And this indicates, the author concluded, that "if all workers who prefer to unionize (one-third of the unorganized work force) were organized, the size of the labor movement would nearly double."[11] And this without compulsory union membership provisions!

The Business Cycle and Union Growth

The priority given to economic performance by both unions and workers alike suggests that union membership will tend to fluctuate in accordance with the economic achievements of unions—with their success in getting "more, now" through collective bargaining.

---

[10]Thomas A. Kochan, "How American workers view Labor Unions," *Monthly Labor Review,* Vol. 102, No. 4, April 1979, p. 23.
[11]*Ibid.,* p. 30.

Obviously, economic conditions are among the vital factors affecting a union's economic performance. Let us see, then, how fluctuations in economic activity affect union activity and union membership. Let us see the relationship between the growth of market-oriented business unions and the business cycle.

It is often supposed that union membership behaves counter-cyclically, with membership expanding in depression and falling off or stabilizing during boom. The reasoning behind this analysis is obvious—it assumes that poverty and depression and the fear of unemployment (if not the actual experience of it) are just the economic circumstances which turn people to unions, in a desperate effort to remedy their situation. And conversely, this line of reasoning leads to the conclusion that, during prosperous times, when jobs are plentiful and wages good, workers will see nothing to be gained by joining unions and union membership will level off or decline.

On the face of it, this argument is plausible enough. And the fact that the great union expansion of the 1930's began during the worst depression the United States ever weathered lends it impressive support.

But reality is almost the direct opposite of this. With certain interesting exceptions, such as that noted above (which can be explained in part as an *aftermath* of depression), union membership tends generally to move *with* rather than counter to the business cycle; it tends to rise in prosperity and fall in depression. The reason? Prosperity gives the union its most favorable opportunity for effective union performance, its best chance to pay off for the members.

In other words, to paraphrase a well-known chestnut, "What's good for General Motors is good for organized labor." And this is literally, as well as figuratively, true. In 1973, for example, while General Motors (and the rest of the auto industry) reached record levels of production and profits, the United Auto Workers gained over 150,000 members. What better measure could we have of the *mutual* interests of market-oriented unions and business firms?

This comes about for a number of reasons. The relative scarcity of workers and the relative plenty of jobs characteristic of prosperity give unions extra bargaining power—a seller's market for labor, in other words. This not only enables unions to press for greater gains than usual, but increases their probability of winning them as well. The existence of the seller's market also makes the threat of a strike more serious, for replacing strikers becomes more difficult. And finally, when there is a seller's market for labor, there will be a seller's market for the goods and services of employers. (In fact, the causal relationship runs the other way; the demand for labor is derived from the demand for the employer's product.) Far from making employers more adamant in bargaining, these circumstances tend to make them more willing to compromise. Employers are likely first to be in a better financial position to meet union demands (that is, able to *afford* bigger concessions than at any other time during the cycle), and second, to be anxious to maintain production and thus to accept fairly high costs rather than see it interrupted. Although as a result of the superior earnings that come with prosperity employers are better equipped than usual to engage in a protracted struggle with unions, employers in a competitive industry are likely to put a very high priority on maintaining production without interruption. Perhaps nothing will bring management to terms more rapidly than to see a competitor in full operation while its own plant is shut down by a strike. For this means that the competitor is not only making money while the strike-bound employer is shut down, but, in all likelihood, also capturing customers who may never return. For these reasons, then, the employer's willingness to settle in order to avoid a strike, and the union's ability to make economic gains, tend to be at a peak, rather than a low, during prosperity.

This point was most clearly made by Leland Hazard, late vice president and general counsel of the Pittsburgh Plate Glass Company, when he said:

> The factors which move the more influential segments of industrial management to a wage decision are: (1) the compulsion to maintain production, (2) the need to maintain a feasible price, and (3) the *sine qua non* profit ... Production, price and profit—*And the greatest of these is production.*[12]
>
> ...A customer (big and scarce) lost for lack of production is a loss the finality of which impresses management more than the immediate inability to increase a price to reflect a wage increase, and more than the threat that wages will presently absorb too much of profits. The time will come when the price *can* be increased, the engineers will find a way ... to increase the productivity to offset the wage. But a lost customer—that sad event—leaves a manager inconsolable.[13]
>
> ...It is obvious that the compulsion to maintain uninterrupted production will be a more potent factor in wage determination on the upswing of the business cycle than on the downswing ... on the nether side (downswing) of the cycle an interruption will be less devastating to a customer ... because alternative sources of supply are available.[14]

And, conversely, during depression or recession the combination of a buyer's market for labor with its attendant advantage to the em-

---

[12]Leland Hazard, "Wage Theory: A Management View," in George W. Taylor and Frank C. Pierson, eds., *New Concepts in Wage Determination* (New York: McGraw-Hill, 1957), p. 32.
[13]*Ibid.*, p. 45.
[14]*Ibid.*, p. 48.

ployer; the likelihood that facilities are not being fully utilized anyhow; and the facts that interruption of production is not likely to inconvenience a customer who is not ordering anyhow, that there is little economic fat to give to the union, and that workers who realize that they may be readily replaced by unemployed workers are less likely to risk strike action than ones who are confident of the difficulty of finding replacements—all combine to make periods of depressed economic activity difficult ones in which to improve the worker's economic lot, through collective bargaining or otherwise.

Thus, we find ourselves faced with the fact that a union's ability to deliver the goods, economically speaking, and its ability to reach prospective members where it counts—in the pocketbook—are directly affected by economic conditions.

And though it is doubtless true that workers' economic position will improve during prosperity whether they are unionized or not, there is at least some significant evidence that members of the biggest and/or most powerful unions receive gains above and beyond those of nonunion workers. In any case, unions tend to take the credit for improvements accruing to workers, and to the extent that this is accepted by employees, successful negotiations are perhaps the best organizing appeal there is.

The theory we have been developing here gets substantial support when we look at changes in union membership in manufacturing from 1962 to 1978. First, under the stimulus of an expanding economy and the Vietnam War, union membership in manufacturing rose from 8 million in 1962 to 9.2 million in 1968, in part because a large proportion of union contracts in the manufacturing industries contained a union-shop provision. Indeed, during this period, the increase of membership in manufacturing outpaced that in both nonmanufacturing and government.

But then, under the impact of the 1974–1975 recession, the most severe since World War II, unions in manufacturing lost more than a million members, falling from 9,144,000 to 8,119,000 in just four years.

And 1980 looked like a rerun of 1975—by June 1980, nearly 240,000 auto workers were on indefinite layoff; 60,000 on temporary layoff; and a total of nine automotive plants had closed.[15] In the steel industry, also hard-hit by foreign competition and the slump in auto production, more than 60,000 workers had been furloughed.[16] That this will have an adverse effect on union membership in these industries seems inescapable.

[15]*The New York Times,* June 21, 1980, p. 1.
[16]*The New York Times,* June 19, 1980, p. D 4.

Communist Union Growth

In a predominately market-oriented labor movement such as we have in the United States, unions with a primarily ideological or political orientation, such as communist-dominated unions, tend to have a distinctive appeal largely for those who are dissatisfied with the operation of the economic system and want to replace it with something else rather than work within the existing framework. So far as economic circumstances contribute toward receptiveness to such views, one would expect that the left-wing unions would attract the largest number of followers in times of economic depression, when the tangible rewards of our economic system are at a minimum, and the smallest numbers in periods of prosperity. To put it another way, one would expect membership in communist-dominated unions to move in the opposite direction from the business cycle (in a counter-cyclical pattern), rather than to follow it as membership in the business unions tends to.

The experience of communist-dominated unions in the past forty-five years or so substantially confirms this view. The depression of the 1930's, which at its depth found between 20 and 25 percent of the labor force unemployed, and many not just for months but for years, was a period of intense activity on the part of communists in the labor movement. And by the end of World War II, they had reached a peak strength, aided by the unusual circumstance of the United States' wartime alliance with Russia.

But the postwar prosperity apparently had a detrimental impact on communist influence in the labor movement. While no accurate figures are available on the membership of either the Communist Party in the United States or its strength among union members, it seems hardly coincidental that during this period the *Daily Worker,* the official newspaper of the Communist Party, was forced by dwindling sales to change to *The Worker* (bi-weekly), and that of some eleven unions expelled from the CIO in 1949–1950 on grounds of communist domination, only two were left as separate unions by 1980.

Indeed, it appears that, to survive, the communist-dominated unions have been forced, for tactical reasons, to compete on the business unions' own terms of delivering the goods—economically speaking.

The Economics of Organizing

Whether or not workers join unions depends on two types of factors—those which affect the willingness of workers to join unions and those which affect the organizing activity of the unions themselves. For while it is true that many of the elements that affect the workers' willingness to join unions are beyond the control of the unions, it is also true that it is not enough simply for workers to be favorably disposed toward unions. New members are more often acquired through organizing campaigns than from would-be members knocking at the union door. Unions are well aware that salesmanship is often necessary to convert a potential member into an active one, and substantial resources, both in time and money, go into organizing campaigns.

An example of this may be found in the Teamsters Union financial reports for the two calendar years 1973 and 1974. During this two-year period, organizing-campaign expenses amounted to over $14 million, or approximately one-sixth of the total operating expenses of the national union (and this figure gives no idea of how much more may have been spent by local unions in the same organizing drives).[17] And yet, for all this expense, total membership of the Teamsters increased by only 118,613.[18] In this case, the net cost of a "permanent" addition to the Teamsters Union membership ran in the vicinity of $120 per capita—roughly double what it had been in 1965.[19]

Since organizing is an expensive process that draws heavily on a union's financial and personnel resources, it tries to utilize them economically and to spend them where they will do the most good. This means deciding *which* workers are the critical ones to win over to the union cause.

As we have seen, "Labor organization emerges among employees who have strategic market or technological positions. They have bargaining power. They can make it hurt. These strategic employees may be regarded as 'points of infection' or 'growth cones' . . . for the spread of labor organization."[20] In organizing a plant or store, therefore, a union doesn't pay equal attention to all workers, but tries to concentrate its energies where they will be most effective. In retail trades, for example, crucial occupations *within* the store have been the meat-cutters (in supermarkets) or shoe clerks, or appliance salesmen (in department stores). In the clothing industries, the cutters were the first to be organized.

In each case, the crucial occupations have been the first to be organized because they had a skill that was hard to replace, and accordingly, had substantial bargaining power. They had status—their skill, bargaining power, and superior earnings led other workers to look up

Dud?

---

[17]See *The International Teamster,* April 1974, p. 24, and May 1975, p. 24.

[18]U.S. Department of Labor, "Labor Union and Employee Association Membership, 1974," *op. cit.,* p. 7.

[19]*The International Teamster* (March 1966), p. 28.

[20]John T. Dunlop, "The Development of Labor Organization: A Theoretical Framework," in Richard A. Lester and Joseph Shister, eds., *Insights into Labor Issues* (New York: Macmillan, 1948), p. 180.

to and respect them; when they join the union, they set an example for others to follow. In short, the skilled and strategically located worker is *still* the first to be organized, just as he was a century and a half ago.

In any discussion of union organizing tactics, it should be recognized that, historically at least, persuading *workers* that they should join the union was only one of the methods of organizing unions. Many unions in the past have found it both quicker and less expensive to focus their energies on persuading the *employer* to recognize the union—without consulting the employees directly involved; hence, the so-called "sweetheart agreement," bitterly criticized as undemocratic, in which the union induced the employer to recognize it directly as representative of his employees, with the result that the new members often learned of their membership by an announcement from the employer. In such cases, the union may seek help from such strategic workers as the teamsters, who may not be employed at the plant or store being organized, but simply may handle its deliveries. In this case, the organizer's tactics may involve persuading teamsters to come to his assistance by exerting pressure on the employer to recognize the union as representative of his workers.[21]

There are other variables that affect the costs of organizing. Such factors as high labor turnover or the scattering of workers among many employers or over wide geographic areas can impede union growth by causing high per capita organizing costs.

High labor turnover is expensive for unions because it forces them, in the absence of a union shop or closed shop, to organize two or three workers to maintain a single membership. One of the great advantages to the union of compulsory union membership lies in the fact that it is such an efficient and inexpensive organizing device. And where a union is trying to organize industries characterized by many small and widely scattered plants, an organizer may have to visit many plants just to contact a few hundred workers. Instead of meeting with large groups of workers, the organizer may have to recruit workers almost individually, with the result that productivity is low and organizing costs are high.

Unfortunately for the unions, both high labor turnover and wide dispersal of labor are characteristic of the service industries, in which the principal expansion of the labor force is occurring. Added to the problem of worker indifference or hostility to them, unions are faced with the hard fact that the major unorganized sectors of the economy are inherently costly to organize. So far as organizing is concerned, the rich veins have already been tapped, the cream has been skimmed off the top, and only the high-cost reserves remain.

---

[21]See Marten S. Estey, "The Strategic Alliance as a Factor in Union Growth," *Industrial and Labor Relations Review*, October 1955, pp. 41–53.

Motivation for Organizing in the Private Sector

But the union decision to invest in an organizing drive is more than a matter of weighing the costs of organizing against the probable future revenue to be obtained from the new member; it is more than a question of imperialistic motives, the desire to expand simply for expansion's sake. Thus, while there is doubtless an important element of empire-building in the organizing activities of any union (as well as an element of the old-fashioned missionary bringing the gospel to the heathen), the motivation of union organizing drives cannot be properly appreciated if we ignore the fact that one of the most urgent and persistent pressures on unions in the private sector to expand membership is the presence, in a partially organized industry, of nonunion firms which act as an obstacle to the improvement of the wages, hours, and working conditions of union members.

So long as there are nonunion firms in an industry, the improvement of union wages tends to create a differential within the industry which works to the competitive disadvantage of unionized employers. Eventually a point is reached at which the differential is more than they can absorb or offset, and their resistance to further gains is stiffened and/or they are threatened by a loss of business to lower-cost competitors. In either case, the unions are hurt. Accordingly, unions are under continuous pressure, quite aside from any imperialistic motives, to organize nonunion firms to remove the barrier to bargaining gains for their present members by taking wages out of competition. And since economic gains may be the *sine qua non* for holding their existing membership, expansion may, in some cases, be almost literally a matter of institutional survival. Under such circumstances, the union may look on the nonunion worker not simply as a prospective customer to be wooed by effective salesmanship, but also as an unethical competitor who is jeopardizing the welfare of the union. With such a view, the democratic right of the nonunion worker to join or not is easily lost sight of, as the union resorts to any method available to it to rid itself of competition.

Motivation for Organization in the Public Sector

The competitive pressure which is of such fundamental importance in constantly pushing unions in the private sector to expand is generally not a significant factor in the public sector, but there is an analogous pressure to expand the coverage of a collective bargaining agreement arising out of the need for equitable treatment of all employees of a single public employer, if not in terms of wage levels, at least in terms of wage increases.

How great is the pressure both for equity (and the various ways equity may be defined) and for the expansion of the number of employees covered by a single agreement is vividly illustrated by the negotiations between the City of New York and its municipal employees' unions in the summer of 1980. After thirty-two unions representing 200,000 nonuniformed employees, negotiating as a coalition, won a wage increase of 8 percent in mid-June, a coalition of eight unions of uniformed personnel sought a 10 percent increase, while the city strove to get them to accept the 8 percent it had granted the nonuniformed employees.[22]

And one expert on unionism in the public sector has suggested that "the experience in the public sector offers strong evidence for the general proposition that once a substantial proportion of employees in any political jurisdiction . . . organize for collective bargaining under the protection of a collective bargaining statute, all other eligible employees of that same public employer will soon follow suit in order to protect their proportionate share of public expenditures."[23]

Teamsters Union Growth—
A Case in Point

This analysis of the factors which influence workers to join unions is helpful not only in understanding overall trends in union membership but also in shedding light on the trends of union membership in particular industries. We have seen, for example, that the Teamsters Union in the decade 1964–1974 gained more members than any other union, despite a continuous storm of controversy about its leadership. A brief look at the environment in which the Teamsters operate suggests that there are sound objective reasons for their position as a growth union.

The Teamsters deal, first of all, with a segment of the labor force which seems likely to find unionism attractive. In their basic jurisdiction in the trucking industry, the proportion of workers who consider themselves permanently in the employee category is fairly high; opportunities for self-employment, while still an important factor in trucking, appear to be declining as costs of equipment rise. There are few women

[22]*The New York Times,* July 1, 1980, pp. 1, B2.
[23]Ronald Donovan, as quoted in John F. Burton, Jr., "The Extent of Collective Bargaining in the Public Sector," *Public-Sector Bargaining,* Benjamin Aaron, Joseph R. Grodin and James L. Stern, eds. Industrial Relations Research Association Series (Washington, D.C.: The Bureau of National Affairs, Inc., 1979), p. 37, *n.* 58.

and relatively few white-collar workers—few of the workers for whom unions may be a questionable investment.

At the same time, economic factors have been favorable to Teamster growth. Their bargaining power is unquestionable. The economic leverage and bargaining power flowing from their strategic position is almost unrivaled. Because a large and increasing proportion of all goods is moved to and from the factory or store by truck, the Teamsters control a strategic bottleneck, with which they can inflict great costs on an employer at little cost to themselves.

They are in an expanding industry, with all the economic advantages that entails. In addition, to take the greatest possible advantage of economic growth of the trucking industry and to overcome the adverse effects of nonunion competition, the union has been moving for several years toward national collective bargaining for intercity freight and other segments of the Teamsters' jurisdiction.

The collective impact of these factors is almost entirely favorable— a labor force which includes relatively few groups resistant to unions, ample bargaining power and economic leverage, and the stimulus of economic growth in the industry—with all that implies concerning satisfactory performance by the union.

The State and the Unions

6

This chapter deals with what is commonly referred to as public policy with regard to union activity. Public policy is not a synonym for public opinion about labor issues, although it is often influenced by it. Public policy refers to *government* policy with respect to unions and their behavior.

Public policy in the field of labor is expressed in a variety of ways—in law, in administrative rulings and interpretations, in "guidelines," and even in decisions as to how and when to intervene in particular disputes or problems.

In the present chapter, we have generally confined our attention to the most basic expression of public policy, the law. The law provides the general ground rules of the game for unions and for union-management relations; it establishes the general boundaries between proper and improper conduct. And, as in other games, the rules are constantly evolving and being re-evaluated.

But despite the dynamic nature of public policy, it is important to realize the extent to which the basic issues involved in public policy persist. While the problems with which public policy deals vary unceasingly, these variations are often simply different manifestations of an historic issue. Questions such as how to balance the conflicting rights of nonunion workers, union members, and the public at large; what methods unions should be permitted in pursuing their objectives; and even where to draw the line between public and private determination of labor relations problems are among the persistent and recurring issues of public policy which have been with us since the Cordwainer's case in 1806 and for which new answers have to be found as new developments occur.

Although the development of public policy for labor relations appears here as a number of discrete events, each occurring at a particular time and place, it would be a mistake to assume that each turn of policy, each major court decision, and each major piece of legislation was simply a response to the circumstances and pressures of the moment. A more realistic and useful view is that each of these events represents the culmination of a long period of concern and experimentation and that the development of public policy is a continuous process of evolution and adaptation to changing economic and social facts and needs.

Common Versus Statute Law

In the United States, the law of labor relations has been expressed over the years in two basic forms, common law and statute law. American common law, which is an outgrowth of the English legal system, is sometimes referred to as unwritten law because it is in part based on custom and precedent. In general, however, it is more accurate to think of common law as judge-made law, consisting of court decisions interpreting existing laws or deciding issues not yet subject to statute law. In any case, the volumes of court decisions in the nearest law library are mute evidence that common law is amply documented.

In contrast to common law, statute law is law enacted by legislative bodies and expressed in a formal document. It includes the laws passed by the Congress of the United States and those passed by the various state and municipal legislative bodies, though we will be primarily concerned here with federal rather than state or municipal legislation.

One widely held view is that in the field of social policy, including union activity and labor relations, the common law has tended to be more conservative and less adaptable to changing economic and social conditions than statute law, both in England and in the United States. And certainly, as we look at the development of American public policy toward unions, it is apparent that, broadly speaking, so long as public policy was shaped primarily by the courts, say from 1800 to the 1920's, it was generally restrictive and restraining, while since the 1920's, it has been predominantly expressed in statute law and has been generally less restrictive and more encouraging of union activity, at least until the passage of the Taft-Hartley and Landrum-Griffin Acts in 1947 and 1959, respectively. To explain this dichotomy it is generally noted that legislative bodies, being composed of elected officials, are more likely to reflect and be sensitive to public opinion than are the courts, whose officials are generally appointed, and that by the very nature of its functions, the legislative branch of government is bound to be more innovative than the judicial branch.

But perhaps the more fundamental reason for the shift in the 1920's from a restrictive to an encouraging legal climate for unions is to be found in the long-term shifts in the composition of the labor force. During most of the nineteenth century, we were still predominantly an agricultural society. More than half the population was still on farms or in small towns, and was traditionally anticollectivist and antiunion. By 1920, a great migration from the farm to the factory and from the country to the city had taken place, climaxed by the impetus given it by World War I. The voting population had become a predominantly urban and industrial one, with the problems, interests, and outlook of industrial workers and urbanites. *This,* in the last analysis, is what underlies the shift in public policy; this explains the timing of that shift.

The Conspiracy Doctrine

Thirty years after the Declaration of Independence, another historic event took place in Philadelphia—the first American court case involving the right of workers to belong to unions, engage in collective bargaining, and resort to economic action to gain their objectives. But the decision of the court in this case—the Philadelphia Cordwainers (shoemakers) Case of 1806—was no declaration of independence for the industrial worker; ironically enough the outcome was just the opposite, for the court, depending on English common law, which from the middle of the fourteenth century had treated as illegal all attempts to raise wages by "concerted" (i.e., organized) action, noted that "a combination of workmen to raise their wages may be considered in a twofold point of view: one is to benefit themselves . . . the other to injure those who do not join their society. The rule of the law condemns both," and proceeded to find the cordwainers guilty of conspiracy.[1]

This did not mean, of course, that it was illegal for the individual worker to seek a wage increase; what was illegal, and what constituted the conspiracy, was the mere fact of *collective* action—quite irrespective of the facts that the objective of higher wages was itself legal and that no methods unlawful *per se* were used.

The hard line taken in the Cordwainers case was subsequently eased in the case of *Commonwealth* v. *Hunt* in 1842, when what would now be called the rule of reason was applied to union activity. Here the judge ruled that, for a union to be guilty of conspiracy, either its objective or the means used to reach it must be criminal or unlawful. Thus, the court no longer regarded unions as necessarily synonymous with conspiracy,

---

[1]Benjamin J. Taylor and Fred Whitney, *Labor Relations Law,* 2nd Ed. (Englewood Cliffs, N.J.: Prentice-Hall, 1975), p. 18.

but acknowledged that they might have beneficial as well as adverse public impact.

Seen in retrospect, the Cordwainers case is perhaps of chiefly symbolic interest (although the charge of conspiracy continued to be a significant issue in court cases involving labor until the 1880's). Quite apart from its specific content, it is significant as the case that ushered in what we describe here as the common-law era of public policy toward organized labor and set the essentially restrictive tone which was to prevail, with variations and modifications, for more than a century.

Equally important is the fact that the Cordwainers case presents in microcosm the fundamental issues with respect to the rights of workers and unions with which the makers of public policy have grappled from that day to this. Thus, while their specific manifestations (and the policy positions related to them) have changed, the basic issues—of the proper balance between property rights and human rights, between the rights and freedoms of union members and those of nonunion workers, and between the rights of the worker to organize and bargain collectively and the rights of the public at large—are as crucial today as they were one hundred and seventy-five years ago. The Cordwainers case is a vivid reminder that it is not so much the problems and issues that change as it is our concepts of them and our views as to how they should be dealt with.

The Injunction

As the conspiracy doctrine dwindled in importance, unions found themselves confronted with another legal obstacle—the injunction, or court order to cease and desist from some specified action such as a strike, a boycott, or picketing. Violation of the order, of course, is contempt of court and punishable accordingly; this is what put the teeth into the injunction.

In labor relations, as in other uses, the injunction is primarily a preventive device, developed to cope with the fact that in many situations, damages or losses resulting from certain actions cannot be adequately compensated for, either because what is damaged or destroyed cannot be replaced, or because the dollar value of the loss cannot be properly calculated. If a hundred-year-old tree in front of your house is about to be cut down by the city in a street-widening program, an injunction (if you can get it) is clearly preferable to trying to replace the tree after it is cut down, or trying to estimate its dollar value. Similarly, employers have turned to the courts for injunctions against strikes, picketing, and boycotts on the grounds that these union activities threatened to cause irreparable or incalculable damage, not necessarily to their physical property, but more generally to their property right to do business and make profits.

In the United States, the use of injunctions in labor disputes began in the 1880's, when they were issued by a number of state courts. The labor injunction received its greatest impetus, however, in 1894, when the federal government obtained an injunction to end the famous Pullman strike and was upheld by the Supreme Court in its contention that the injunction was a legitimate measure for the control of labor disputes. After this decision, the use of the labor injunction became widespread and continued so for nearly forty years, until the passage of the Norris-LaGuardia Act in 1932.

The injunction was an effective way of controlling unions, for by preventing strikes, picketing, and boycotts, and thus restricting or depriving unions of the use of their principal economic weapons, it severely limited their power and effectiveness in collective bargaining. Union leaders accordingly viewed the injunction with particular distaste, maintaining that "no weapon has been used with such disastrous effects against trade unions as has the injunction."[2] One impartial authority has concluded that from the 1890's to the 1930's the injunction was used "to assist in defeating most of the more important strikes . . . to prevent the successful spreading of labor boycotts . . . and . . . to prevent organizing activities."[3]

Aside from its impact on unions, an important aspect of the widespread use of the injunction during this period was that it put the courts increasingly into a central role in labor disputes and further enhanced their part in determining public policy in *practice*—a fact which led to bitter union complaints of "government by injunction."

Increasing doubts about the wisdom of such extensive judicial intervention in labor disputes (to say nothing of questions as to judicial impartiality or lack of it), plus concern over an apparent trend toward increasingly restrictive injunctions and the granting of temporary injunctions without benefit of hearings, eventually led to the Norris-LaGuardia Act of 1932, which imposed substantial restrictions on their use and effectively reduced the role of the federal courts in labor disputes.

While the use of the injunction was in some degree restored when the Taft-Hartley Act made it available for use by the federal government, and while the Norris-LaGuardia Act does not control the issuance of injunctions by state courts, the fact remains that since Norris-LaGuardia, the injunction has been of limited significance in labor disputes in interstate commerce.

---

[2]John Mitchell, former president of the United Mine Workers, as quoted in Harry A. Millis and Royal E. Montgomery, *Organized Labor* (New York: McGraw-Hill, 1945), p. 631.
[3]*Loc. cit.*

Antitrust Law

Almost at the same time that the injunction was being turned into a device for curbing union power, another, though probably less effective, restraint on the unions' use of economic measures was developed when the courts, by interpretation, extended the application of the antitrust laws from business firms—for which they were presumably designed—to unions.

The original federal antitrust law, of course, was the Sherman Antitrust Act of 1890, which prohibits both "combinations in restraint of trade" and "attempts to monopolize trade" and provides that offenders shall be punished by fine or imprisonment or both and be subject to triple damages. Unlike the injunction, the Sherman Act is not preventive. Its effectiveness lies in the prospects that punishments after the fact will discourage future violations, but it is obviously a less direct restraint on union action than the injunction.

Although a number of lower courts had already applied the Sherman Act to unions, the key decision so far as organized labor was concerned was that of the Supreme Court in the Danbury Hatters case (*Loewe* v. *Lawlor*) in 1908. During the course of an organizing campaign at the Loewe Hat Company, the United Hatters union had applied economic pressure on the company by persuading the American Federation of Labor to urge union members throughout the country to refrain from buying Loewe's hats—in short, to boycott the company. The question before the Court was whether this boycott, which had been followed by a decline in the company's interstate sales, constituted a restraint of trade prohibited by the Sherman Act. The Supreme Court ruled that the boycott *was* a violation of the Act and thus opened the way to the use of the Sherman Act against labor's major economic weapon, the strike (although, in fact, there was no major case of a strike being found in violation of the Sherman Act until the 1920's).

Shortly after the Danbury Hatters decision, the Sherman Act was amended by the passage of the Clayton Act of 1914, Section 6 of which specified, among other things, that "Nothing contained in the anti-trust laws shall be construed to forbid the existence and operation of labor . . . organizations . . . nor shall such organizations, or the members thereof, be held or construed to be illegal combinations or conspiracies in restraint of trade, under the anti-trust laws."[4] Union leaders were elated, for they believed that Section 6 clearly and unmistakably removed them from the restrictions of the Sherman Act and left them free once more

[4]Taylor and Whitney, *op. cit.,* p. 50.

to use their economic weapons without fear of legal action. Indeed, Samuel Gompers himself hailed the Clayton Act as an "Industrial Magna Charta."

Labor's elation, however, proved short-lived. For when the Clayton Act was tested in the courts, the judicial interpretation was that Section 6 had not changed the fundamental fact that it was the *activities* of a union that determined whether or not it was in violation of the antitrust law. The Duplex Printing case, in 1921, which paralleled Danbury Hatters to the extent of involving the same economic weapon, the secondary boycott, offered an ideal test case of the Clayton Act. And the Supreme Court, as in the earlier case, found that the *action* violated the Sherman Act. In short, nothing had been changed by the Clayton Act; in terms of the antitrust laws, unions were back where they had been in 1908, when the Danbury Hatters decision was rendered.

Indeed, they were worse off, for between the Danbury and Duplex decisions, the federal courts, at least, had applied the antitrust laws only to secondary boycotts and to strikes in a single industry, the railroads. After Duplex, however, the Supreme Court found strikes in manufacturing and in coal mining also to be in restraint of trade.

So far as the Sherman Act was concerned, labor's real Magna Charta came in 1940 and 1941, when the long record of judicial decisions placing unions under the restrictions of the antitrust laws was reversed in three key cases, the Apex case, the Milk-Wagon Drivers case, and the Hutcheson case. All legal technicalities aside, the basic fact is that in these three cases, the Supreme Court held that, even where they reduced the flow of goods in interstate commerce, strikes, boycotts, and picketing no longer violated the antitrust laws if the restraint of trade was an *incidental* consequence of the union's pursuit of its primary objective of winning a labor dispute. Unions thus found themselves virtually free to use their economic weapons with impunity. Only in the case of collusion, where a union together with an employer acted to restrain trade or monopolize an industry, was union activity *per se* still subject to the antitrust laws.

Though these key decisions were handed down nearly forty years ago, in the first bloom of the New Deal, they stood basically unchanged as the law of the land until 1965, when the Supreme Court, in the Pennington case, found the United Mine Workers in violation of the Sherman Act on the grounds that it had acted collusively with employers to drive certain competitors out of business—a position reinforced by the Court's 1975 decision in the Connell case.

Thus the Court's interpretation of the law continues to play a significant role in shaping public policy with regard to the application of the antitrust laws to labor organizations.

Railway Labor Act

The transition from common law to statue law as the chief instrument of public policy with respect to unions and collective bargaining was, of course, a long, drawn-out process, reflecting both the changing economic and social structure and the many preliminary experiments and attempts at statute law. It is convenient, nevertheless, to resort to a sort of historical shorthand and use some particular event or date to mark the turning point when common law was superseded by statue law as the primary source of public labor policy. With these qualifications, the appropriate turning point is the Railway Labor Act of 1926, which, although not the first federal statute to deal with the rights of workers to join unions, was historic because it was the first of its kind to pass the scrutiny of the Supreme Court.

The Railway Labor Act may be viewed both as an end and a beginning. With its own antecedents in such earlier experiments in federal protection of union activity as the Erdman Act of 1898 (declared unconstitutional in 1908) and the National War Labor Board of 1918 (many policies of which were subsequently incorporated into the Wagner Act in 1935), it marked the culmination of more than a quarter century of efforts to secure effective federal legislation in the area of labor relations.

More important, it laid much of the groundwork for the Wagner Act and the Taft-Hartley Act, which provide the basic legal framework in which today's labor-management relations are conducted. The Railway Labor Act thus marks the transition in labor relations, not only from common law to statute law but also from a public policy of opposition to one of acceptance of unionism and collective bargaining.

Although there is a popular tendency to identify this historic change in the national labor policy with Franklin Delano Roosevelt and the New Deal, it is an interesting footnote to political history that in fact the shift was initiated under Republican administrations. In 1926, when the Railway Labor Act was passed, Calvin Coolidge was president, while another Republican administration, that of Herbert Hoover, was the one during which the Norris-LaGuardia Act became law in 1932. Clearly, our present labor policy cannot be regarded simply as a Democratic legacy.

The Railway Labor Act of 1926 not only established that "Employees shall have the right to organize and bargain collectively through representatives of their own choosing," but also took steps to ensure the effectiveness of this right in practice, by prohibiting employers from interfering in any way with the organization of their employees and by requiring them to bargain with the unions thus selected. This, in brief, is the essence of present-day labor policy.

But the Act itself was only one side of the coin, for as we have seen, previous attempts at federal legislation in industrial relations had been nullified by adverse court decisions. The other half of the coin, therefore, is the Texas and New Orleans case of 1930, in which the Supreme Court upheld the constitutionality of the Act and confirmed that the terms of the statute were in fact legitimate and proper expressions of public policy, although, of course, they applied only to railroads and not to interstate commerce generally.

Norris-LaGuardia Act

The Norris-LaGuardia Act, passed in 1932, is generally referred to as the anti-injunction act because of the elaborate restrictions it places upon the use of injunctions in labor disputes, with the objective of taking the disputes out of the hands of the federal courts, for all practical purposes, and leaving them to be settled by the parties themselves. Norris-LaGuardia, in a sense, was the logical public policy sequel to the Railway Labor Act, for while the latter had established the principle that union activity should be free from *employer* interference, Norris-LaGuardia substantially freed union activity from *court* interference. Federal courts were forbidden to issue either temporary or permanent injunctions in labor disputes, except in "strict conformity" with the provisions of the Act. No peaceful or nonfraudulent union activity, including strikes and picketing, was subject to injunction. And in cases where the issuance of injunctions was not forbidden outright, the procedures and criteria for imposing an injunction were spelled out in detail in the law rather than being left up to the judgment of the individual court.

In addition to thus defining and limiting the jurisdiction of the courts in labor disputes, the Act also made illegal the infamous "yellow-dog" contract—a contract, signed as a condition of employment, in which the employee agreed not to join a union on penalty of discharge—so called because only a "yellow dog" would take a job subject to such conditions. But since employment pressures *did* force many workers to accept such terms, Norris-LaGuardia was a part of the trend to protect employees against such interference.

While the Norris-LaGuardia Act forbade yellow-dog contracts, it merely extended to interstate commerce in general a protection first provided employees in the Railway Labor Act in 1926. And the Railway Labor Act, in turn, is noteworthy in this respect because it was the first *federal* statute to ban yellow-dog contracts, although some fifteen states had enacted such legislation as early as the 1890's.

NIRA

In 1933 came the first of the New Deal laws to deal with labor relations—the National Industrial Recovery Act, or NIRA. Legally speaking, the NIRA was schizophrenic, for it contained both the famous Section 7(a), which extended into interstate commerce generally the labor policies laid down in the Railway Labor Act, and provisions exempting from the antitrust laws business practices which complied with the NIRA codes for regulating prices and production.

Although the NIRA was declared unconstitutional in May 1935, after less than two years of existence, it nonetheless made a lasting contribution to public policy, since the interpretations and decisions of the numerous cases arising under Section 7(a) became the basis for the unfair labor practice provisions of the Wagner Act, enacted in June 1935, just one month after the decision ending the NIRA.[5]

Wagner Act

From organized labor's point of view, the high-water mark in federal labor legislation was undoubtedly the National Labor Relations Act of 1935, commonly known as the Wagner Act.

Since its immediate predecessor, the NIRA, had been found unconstitutional by the Supreme Court, the status of the Wagner Act, which so closely resembled the labor sections of the NIRA, obviously needed to be settled in court. That test came in 1937, when the Supreme Court heard arguments in the famous Jones and Laughlin case. To the surprise of those who expected it to follow the lines of the NIRA decision, not only was the constitutionality of the Wagner Act upheld, but perhaps even more important in terms of its long-run impact, the Court ruled that the provisions of the Wagner Act applied to manufacturing. Thus, by a broad interpretation of what affected commerce, it initiated an extension of the commerce power of Congress, which not only largely determined the impact of the Wagner Act, but laid the groundwork for a general extension of the regulatory powers of the federal government as well.

It was only after this decision that the full impact of the Wagner Act was felt. Between 1937 and 1947, the year the Wagner Act was amended by the passage of the Taft-Hartley Act, a major change in the industrial-

---

[5]For an interesting discussion of Section 7(a), see Millis and Montgomery, *op. cit.,* pp. 521–522.

relations climate of the United States took place, in large part because of the impact of the Wagner Act. The objective of the law was simple enough—to protect the right of the American worker to join unions if he so desired, free from interference by the employer. It is no secret that the Wagner Act was "pro-labor"—openly and avowedly meant to support and encourage union activity and collective bargaining. Its preamble, in fact, declares United States policy to be that of "encouraging the practice and procedure of collective bargaining" and of "protecting the exercise by workers of full freedom of association, self-organization, and designation of representatives of their own choosing, for the purpose of negotiating the terms and conditions of their employment or other mutual aid or protection."[6] A more concise and open statement of the Congressional intention to support and encourage union activity and collective bargaining would be hard to find.

Let us briefly examine the reasons for the adoption of such a policy. *Why* should Congress be so concerned with promoting collective bargaining? Why should it be necessary to protect the right of workers to join unions?

To correct a widespread misunderstanding of the Wagner Act, we hasten to add that it did not legalize either the existence of unions or the process of bargaining; the right of workers to join unions and to bargain collectively had been established long before the Wagner Act and, in fact, had not been seriously challenged since the demise of the conspiracy doctrine. The Wagner Act was designed to *protect* those rights and make them effective in practice as well as in theory.

The problem to which the Wagner Act addressed itself was the interference with those previously recognized rights. For the fact is that the *right* to join a union was of little or no practical value to a worker so long as an employer was free to fire him or her if it were exercised. And indeed, until the passage of the Wagner Act, this was the fundamental weakness in the civil rights of the industrial worker; economically, the right to join a union was often practically meaningless. Accordingly, the Wagner Act was designed to protect the worker's civil rights by making it illegal for employers to interfere in their use. And indeed, the logic of this is evident (whether you agree with it or not): Why should the exercise of a legal *right* (the right to join a union) be grounds for discharge or discrimination? This was one basis for the Wagner Act, which was in fact a civil-rights law, in the current sense of that phrase.

The Wagner Act was also a recognition of a long-standing economic concept—that the individual worker was unable to bargain on equal

---

[6]The Wagner Act, Findings and Policy, Sec. 1, as quoted in Taylor and Whitney, *op. cit.,* p. 626.

terms with the modern business organization and that without freedom to organize and join unions to restore the balance, economic circumstances and the imperfections of the labor market would often force him or her to accept jobs with undesirably low wages and poor working conditions. Stripped of its elaborate rhetoric, the Wagner Act recognized that competition between workers for jobs tended, like competition in other markets, to force down the price of labor, but that unrestricted competition in the labor market might have adverse effects on income and aggregate demand, especially during depression. Accordingly, by protecting the right to organize and to join unions, competition in the labor market would be reduced and the standards of living of the worker protected.

Finally, the Wagner Act was implicit recognition of the fact that in a country which grants all adults the right to vote and to participate in their government, it is only consistent to provide for democracy in the plant through the mechanism of the labor organization.

Surprisingly enough, only three basic techniques for achieving its objectives were provided in the original Wagner Act. First, the Act prohibited employer conduct designed to interfere with the worker's right to join a union. The nature of this conduct was spelled out in detail in five types of so-called "unfair labor practices" (an inept and confusing term for unfair *employer* practices with respect to labor), which we will describe later in the chapter.

Second, the Act afforded industrial workers and unions a new method of organizing—the secret-ballot election. By means of a secret-ballot election, workers could now *vote* whether or not to be represented by a union. And simple and logical as this technique may seem, it represented a major social innovation, providing a peaceful and orderly way of unionizing, a substitute for organizing by resort to economic pressure.

Finally, the Act established a quasi-judicial agency, the National Labor Relations Board (NLRB), whose function and duty was to enforce and administer the law, to listen to charges of unfair labor practices and to decide on them, and to administer the secret-ballot elections.

Basically, that was all there was to the law. Yet in the ten years between the Jones and Laughlin decision and the enactment of the Taft-Hartley amendments to the Wagner Act, these three provisions virtually revolutionized the conduct of American industrial relations and were a major factor in the vast expansion of union membership from 3.6 million in 1935 to 14 million in 1947. How much of this expansion was due to the Wagner Act, of course, we cannot tell, but it seems inescapable that it was instrumental, and fundamentally so, in bringing about the great change.

Operation of the Act

These three basic provisions have fundamentally changed the theory and practice of industrial relations in the United States. A brief explanation of how they operate follows.[7]

Unfair Labor Practices of Employers

The Wagner Act prohibits employers from engaging in five *types* of practice considered to interfere with workers' rights regarding unions. Since the types of prohibited conduct are defined in rather broad terms, it is up to the National Labor Relations Board in each case to decide whether the particular conduct with which an employer is charged comes under the law and, of course, whether the alleged conduct in fact occurred. Employers are forbidden to:

1. *Interfere, restrain, or coerce employees in their union activities.* Threatening employees with loss of their jobs or loss of benefits if they join a union, threatening to close the plant, and—if a union is organized in it—granting wage increases deliberately timed to prevent unionization are examples of behavior prohibited by the law.

2. *Assist or dominate a labor organization.* "Puppet" unions controlled or supported by the employer are prohibited.

3. *Discriminate in employment for union membership or union activities, or lack of them.* This forbids, for example, demoting or discharging an employee because he or she urged fellow employees to join a union and refusing to hire a qualified applicant for a job because of union membership.

4. *Discriminate for participation in NLRB proceedings.* This is designed to prevent discrimination against employees who bring charges against their employer under this law.

5. *Refuse to bargain collectively with a certified union.* Refusing to put into written form agreements reached with a certified union, giving employees a wage increase larger than that offered to the union, and refusing to deal with union representatives because the employees are out on a lawful strike violate this section of the law.

In unfair labor practice cases, where the Board finds the employer (or now, the union) guilty of a violation of the law, any one of several different actions may result, depending upon the nature of the violation.

[7]This section is based on material in *Federal Labor Laws and Programs,* Bulletin 262/Revised September 1971 (Washington, D.C.: U.S. Department of Labor, Employment Standards Administration, Division of Employment Standards, 1971), pp. 12–15, and 26–28.

If it finds that an employee was discharged because of union membership or union activity (the most frequent unfair labor practice charge),
the Board may order his or her reinstatement, with or without back pay.
If it finds that employer conduct interfered with the worker's decision
to vote for or against a union, the Board may call for a new election. In
other cases, the conduct in question may simply be ordered stopped.

Secret-Ballot Elections

In order for the NLRB to conduct one of the secret-ballot elections
(called a "representation election") by which workers choose whether
they wish to be represented by a union, the union (the customary pe-
titioner for an election) must first demonstrate that there is a bona fide
interest among workers in being represented. By a rule-of-thumb
process, it was early decided that if 30 percent of the workers in a
bargaining unit were interested in having an election and demonstrated
this interest by submitting authorization cards, petitions, or other
means, an election would be held. Similarly, if an employer calls for an
election, the Board must hold a hearing to determine whether it is
justified. Before the election is held, the Board must decide, in conjunction with the employer and the union, which employees are eligible
to vote. The question as to which workers are eligible to vote comes
under the rather misleading heading of "appropriate bargaining unit"—
a term which, in the secret-ballot election process, really involves the
question of the appropriate *voting* unit; it is only after the election is
over and the union has won that it becomes in fact an appropriate
bargaining unit.

The boundaries of the bargaining unit, or voting unit, may vary
widely. It may be limited to a particular group of employees in a particular plant, such as skilled craftsmen, or it may consist of all production
workers in the plant; it may include workers in more than one plant of
the same employer, or it may be so broad as to include workers in plants
of several employers—a so-called multiemployer unit.

In any case, the question of the appropriate bargaining unit may
prove a difficult one. If the employer and the union agree as to the
appropriate unit, well and good; the Board will probably determine that
to be the appropriate unit. But if the employer and union disagree or
if competing unions disagree, as they often do, the decision in practice
then falls on the Board—and its decision as to the appropriate voting
unit may well be, under certain circumstances, the key factor in the final
outcome of the election.

So far as the election itself is concerned, the outcome is decided
by a simple majority of those votes *cast,* rather than a majority of eligible
votes; regardless of the number of employees *eligible* to vote; therefore,
any number greater than 50 percent of the votes *cast* will be decisive.

Although, conceivably, the actions of a small fraction of eligible employees could determine the outcome of an election binding on many workers, in practice nearly 90 percent of those eligible to vote do so; the number who passively acquiesce by "letting George do it" is normally, therefore, quite small. And if a majority of those voting cast their vote for a union, the union is then certified by the Board as the authorized bargaining representative for *all* employees in the bargaining unit. It then becomes the legal duty of the employer to bargain with it; to fail to do so is an unfair labor practice.

But here a caution is in order—the requirement to *bargain* is *not* a requirement to *agree* to the union's demands, either in full or in part. It is simply a duty to negotiate with the union. This point, however, is the source of much confusion at present, for it now involves the question of whether an employer is bargaining in good faith—whether compliance is genuine or only nominal. Indeed, trying to assess that issue is so difficult that the National Labor Relations Board by 1969 had "virtually abandoned [it] . . . altogether."[8]

The National Labor Relations Board

As created by the terms of the Wagner Act, the NLRB is an independent agency of the federal government. It has, however, no independent power to enforce its decisions, and if an employer or union fails to comply with its orders, the Board must ask a U.S. court of appeals for an enforcement decree. If a court decree is issued, failure to comply becomes contempt of court and is punishable accordingly. At the same time, Board decisions are themselves subject to appeal up to and including the Supreme Court.

Although the enforcement of the Wagner Act (as amended by Taft-Hartley and Landrum-Griffin) is one of its primary functions, the Board can deal only with cases submitted to it; charges of unfair labor practices or requests for representation elections must be made to the Board before it can enter a case. Because it is a quasi-judicial agency, the Board's decisions as to whether particular conduct violates the law serve to put flesh on the bare bones of the statute; just as the decisions of the court provide the common law, so the decisions of the NLRB have the force and effect of law. The Board's interpretation of the statute from case to case and from day to day determines the details of public policy; its interpretations are the law of the land so far as labor relations are concerned.

In this situation, it is hardly surprising that the Board's interpretations of the legality of employer and union conduct have often been the center of controversy, or that the Board should be the subject of argu-

---

[8]*Thirty-ninth Annual Report of the National Labor Relations Board, 1974,* p. 151.

ment and debate aimed at modifying its decisions in favor of one interest group or the other. Thus, almost since its creation in 1935, the Board has been accused by employers and employer organizations of being pro-labor, of partisan interpretation of the law in favor of unions.

Less widely realized, perhaps, is that the Board has been almost as vehemently criticized by organized labor. In 1973, for instance, when a majority of the five-man Board were Nixon appointees, the American Federation of Labor complained that under the Nixon Board, the law was being "honed into an instrument whose cutting edge seriously endangers the ability of unions to organize the unorganized and to do an effective job for the members they represent."[9]

And since Board members are presidential appointees, it is not surprising that the appointments should reflect the political leanings and spirit of the administration in office. But quite aside from the evaluation of the tenor of the Board's decisions over the past forty-five years, it should be remembered that the Wagner Act and, no less certainly, the Taft-Hartley Act establish the overall framework within which the Board's decisions and judgments must be made. Taft-Hartley has not significantly changed the basic intent of the Wagner Act, which is to encourage collective bargaining as a process, and unions as institutions. This objective is the statutory mandate within which the Board must operate; it cannot legally do otherwise.

Any fair evaluation of the Board's decisions, therefore, must take this fact into account. The Board can hardly be accused of partisan behavior if the regulations which it is called upon to interpret are essentially pro-labor in the first place. The criteria by which the Board's role would have to be judged are (1) whether its interpretations effectively depart from the intent of Congress when it drafted the law, and (2) whether, within the area of its discretion, it consistently or persistently tips the scales in favor of (say) labor. And, of course, in interpreting a law sections of which were enacted thirty or forty years earlier, the Board increasingly encounters situations which were not taken into consideration when the law was written; in these cases, it may very well have to venture into new policy determinations for which the statute itself gives little if any guidance. And finally, it should be noted that in so controversial an area as labor relations policy, where there are no scientific answers and no pat formulas, the question of what is "sound" or "good" public policy is often, in the last analysis, a question of the values one holds.

Without trying to appraise the content of the Board's decisions, one measure of the Board's performance over the years may be found in the

---

[9]*Report of the Executive Council of the AFL-CIO*, Tenth Convention, Bal Harbour, Florida, 1973, p. 257.

record of cases appealed to the courts for review and enforcement by the Board or by employers and unions contesting the Board's decisions.

The record shows that in forty-five years of operation, the Board's decisions and interpretations have been affirmed in full by both U.S. courts of appeals and the Supreme Court four times as often as they have been set aside.

Of the 7,217 cases referred to courts of appeals in the forty-four years from July 5, 1935 to September 30, 1979, Board orders were affirmed in full in 63.4 percent of the cases, and modified or remanded in another 21.9 percent. They were set aside in only 14.7 percent of the cases.

And of the 226 cases that reached the Supreme Court in this period, it affirmed 60.2 percent of the Board's decisions in full, modified or remanded 23.8 percent, and set aside only 16 percent.[10]

Taft-Hartley Act

The state of the unions in 1947 was remarkably different from what it had been in 1935, the year the Wagner Act was passed. Under the combined stimulus of the Wagner Act and the economic expansion of World War II, union membership had risen more than 10 million, from around 3.6 million to 14 million; unions had penetrated the mass-production industries, and individual unions had grown to unprecedented sizes. Unions had been touched by success beyond their wildest dreams.

This very success, however, stirred a vital nerve in the American character—fear of bigness *per se*. The feeling that labor had become too big and too powerful, and that such power had to be checked and brought under control, gained increasing momentum (no doubt prompted by employers anxious to keep unions from threatening *their* power).

When, on the termination of wartime controls, pent-up energy was released in the form of a wave of strikes, it was the signal for the passage of the Taft-Hartley Act, alternatively described by its advocates as a way of restoring the balance of power between labor and management and by its critics as a "slave-labor" law.

It should be realized from the outset that the Wagner Act was not repealed by the passage of the Taft-Hartley Act; Taft-Hartley is an *amendment* to the Wagner Act, not a replacement or a substitute for it. And the provisions of the Wagner Act, therefore, are still in full force and effect, except as they have been modified or supplemented by the provisions of the Taft-Hartley and Landrum-Griffin Acts.

[10]*Forty-fifth Annual Report of the National Labor Relations Board, 1979*, p. 313.

Quite aside from the specific and detailed differences in the provisions of the Wagner and Taft-Hartley Acts is the fundamental difference in their philosophy and in their relationship to what is presently described as free collective bargaining. The role of government vis-à-vis the collective bargaining process is significantly different in the two laws.

The difference is this: the Wagner Act was designed to encourage collective bargaining and, under specified circumstances, to require it. Once a union had been certified as the representative of the workers in an appropriate bargaining unit, the employer no longer had the option to bargain or not as he saw fit; he was required to bargain, but he was not required to submit to union demands. Furthermore, the terms of the agreement were not regulated; whatever agreement was reached between a union and a company was acceptable under the Wagner Act. Thus, in effect, the role of the government, under Wagner, was to get the parties to the bargaining table and to get the bargaining process under way, and no more. The content of the agreement was not at issue.

With Taft-Hartley, this situation changed. The old requirements to bargain were retained, but now the content of the agreement was subject to regulation; even if both parties wanted it, for example, a closed-shop provision could not be included in a union contract with an employer engaged in interstate commerce. The area of government regulation, in short, was extended from the *process* of collective bargaining to the *terms* of the collective bargaining agreement; it was a step looked on with concern by the devotees of free (unregulated) collective bargaining on both sides of the table.

The stated purpose of the Taft-Hartley Act is brief and to the point, namely, "to provide additional facilities for mediation of labor disputes affecting commerce, to equalize legal responsibilities of labor organizations and employers, and for other purposes."

Unfair Labor Practices of Unions

As a means of equalizing the responsibilities of unions and employers, Congress balanced the unfair labor practice provisions of the Wagner Act (which, as we have seen, regulated *employer* conduct in labor relations) with a set of six categories of unfair labor practices of *unions*.[11] Under Section 8(b) of the law, unions may not:

1. *Restrain or coerce employees* in the exercise of their right to join unions of their own choosing or to refrain from joining a union. This basically parallels the prohibition on employers.

[11]*Federal Labor Laws and Programs,* Bulletin No. 262, *op. cit.,* pp. 15–21.

2. *Cause discrimination for union activities.* This prohibits unions from trying to cause employers to engage in the unfair labor practice of discrimination in their behalf.

3. *Refuse to bargain with an employer* when the union is the certified representative of the workers. This parallels the prohibition on employers.

4. *Engage in secondary boycotts.* Probably the most complex provision in Taft-Hartley, this section is intended to define and regulate the use of an economic weapon of unions and to minimize the use of innocent third parties as tools in disputes between unions and employers.

5. *Charge excessive or discriminatory initiation fees.* What constitutes an excessive or discriminatory fee is left to the judgment of the NLRB.

6. *Featherbed.* Although defined here as causing an employer to pay for services not performed, generally speaking, the problem of featherbedding is not concerned with whether services are performed for pay, but with whether or not they are *necessary.*

In addition to defining these unfair labor practices of unions, Taft-Hartley contained a complex variety of amendments of the Wagner Act such as those detailing regulation of union security practices; providing new regulations with regard to employee elections; providing for damage suits against unions; requiring financial and constitutional reports from unions and non-communist affidavits from their officers; authorizing and, in some cases, requiring the NLRB to use injunctions to prevent unfair labor practices; and establishing the injunction as a means of coping with national emergency strikes. (Some of these provisions, in turn, have since been amended by Title VII of the Landrum-Griffin Act, which contains amendments to Taft-Hartley and is separate and distinct from the main body of the Landrum-Griffin Act.)

Union Security

As it now stands, the *closed shop,* which requires employees to be union members *before* they are hired, is illegal. However, in the building and construction industry, which was the bastion of the closed shop, "prehire" agreements, covering both present and future employees, and requiring union membership after seven days' employment, are permitted.

The *union shop,* in which the employee must join the union within thirty days *after* being hired, may now be negotiated without special formality, except in "right-to-work" states, where state law prohibits both union shops and closed shops.

In addition, even though a union shop exists, neither employees who have been refused union membership nor members who have lost their membership are to be discriminated against—i.e., fired—unless they were refused membership or lost their membership status for refusal to pay dues and/or initiation fees.

Because the "right-to-work" laws are the outgrowth of Section 14(b) of Taft-Hartley (a unique clause that, in cases where they conflict, permits state law to supersede federal law as to the union shop), the fight over the right-to-work issue was focused in 1965 and 1966 on that section. Had it been repealed, as labor urged, the customary priority of federal over state law would have been restored and state right-to-work laws automatically rendered invalid.

Decertification and Deauthorization Elections

To the representation elections provided for in the Wagner Act, Taft-Hartley adds two other types of elections—the decertification election, in which employees vote whether they want to stop being represented by their union, and the deauthorization election, in which they vote whether to continue the right of their union to make a union-shop contract.

Although decertification is doubtless a desirable safeguard for employees dissatisfied with the efficacy of their union, in practice it remains relatively unimportant, despite the fact that the number of decertification cases has more than doubled in the decade 1969–1979. In 1979, for example, of a total of 8,043 conclusive representation elections conducted by the NLRB, only 777, or 9.6 percent, involved decertification. The unions lost in 583 cases, involving 22,088 employees, and won in 194, covering 17,450. But the 22,088 employees that the unions lost the right to represent were equivalent to less than one-tenth of 1 percent of union and association membership in the United States in 1978.

And the 134 deauthorization elections in 1979 constituted only 2.3 percent of all representation elections. Unions' right to make union-shop agreements was withdrawn in 92 cases, involving 3,025 employees, and upheld in 42, covering 2,677.[12]

Labor Disputes

To facilitate the achievement of collective bargaining agreements and to help settle disputes, Taft-Hartley created the Federal Mediation and Conciliation Service (FMCS) as an independent agency and required that,

[12]*Forty-fifth Annual Report of the National Labor Relations Board, op. cit.,* pp. 17–18.

thirty days before the expiration date of any existing contract, the parties to it must notify the FMCS that a labor dispute exists (unless of course they have already reached agreement on a new contract). The point, of course, is to make mediation and conciliation available before a crisis is reached, although the parties are under no obligation to accept FMCS aid.

More dramatic, though probably no more important in the long-run, are the provisions for handling so-called "national-emergency strikes"—strikes which may "imperil the national health or safety." Under this provision, when the president of the United States thinks a national emergency exists or is pending as a result of a strike, he appoints a board to determine the issues in the dispute. After the board reports to him, he directs the attorney general to seek an eighty-day injunction from a United States district court, which requires employees to return (or continue) to work for that period. After sixty days, if the dispute has not been settled, the board of inquiry reports on the state of the dispute and makes public the employer's "last offer." The employees, in secret ballot, vote whether to accept the "last offer." If a settlement has not been reached at the end of eighty days, the injunction expires and the parties are free to return to their strike or lockout, in which case the president is left to recommend further action to Congress.

From 1947 through 1979, the Taft-Hartley injunction was used thirty-two times—an average of once a year. But from 1971 through 1976, there was an unprecedented five years in which the emergency dispute procedure was not utilized at all; whether this marked the beginning of a new trend is an intriguing question.

The number of industries in which emergency disputes have occurred is small: as of June, 1980, only eleven had been involved, with most disputes concentrated in five industries—ten in longshoring, five in aircraft-aerospace, four each in bituminous coal and atomic energy, and three in maritime. The others were copper, steel, and grain elevators (two each), and meatpacking, shipbuilding, and telephones.[13]

From this brief glimpse at the record, it is evident that whether a strike or threatened strike is likely to be classed as a national emergency is to a large extent dependent upon the nature of the industry and upon whether its service or product is really a necessity for which there is no effective substitute and whose use we cannot reasonably delay.

A more important issue, of course, is how effective the Taft-Hartley injunction has been in settling the disputes in which it has been employed. In at least nine cases, strikes occurred or were resumed after the eighty-day injunction had expired. Furthermore, it seems evident,

[13]*National Emergency Disputes under the Taft-Hartley Act, 1947–77,* U.S. Department of Labor, Bureau of Labor Statistics, Report 542, 1978, pp. 1–4.

on the basis of both logic and experience, that the requirement of a secret-ballot vote by employees on whether to accept or reject the employer's "last offer" is a waste of time and an indication of Congress' basic misunderstanding of collective bargaining tactics.

If, as the congressional draftsmen of this provision obviously expected, a secret ballot would give the members the chance to express their true feelings and thus prevent "dictatorial" labor leaders from keeping them out on strike against their wishes, one would expect to find a number of instances where this expectation was realized. In actual practice, however, in *none* of the seventeen cases where a vote was actually held on the employer's "last offer" did the membership vote to accept! The reason, on reflection, seems clear—regardless of whether the members *wanted* the strike (a meaningless term in such a situation), by *rejecting* the employer's "last offer" the workers expect to force him to raise it. And, indeed, in at least five of the cases where the "last offer" was rejected by membership vote, the final settlement *was* higher than the "last offer."

It should be pointed out, of course, that the fact that the president has the *authority* to initiate this procedure is no guarantee that he will use it. In 1952, in order to avert a threatened steel strike, President Truman seized the steel industry rather than invoke the Taft-Hartley Act. And in 1966, President Johnson was criticized in some quarters for failure to utilize the Taft-Hartley injunction in connection with the New York City transit strike in January of that year.

Landrum-Griffin Act

We have noted before that a vital union function is to bring a greater degree of democracy into business organizations by providing employees with a mechanism by which they can participate in the decisions regarding their terms of employment. Paradoxically, as unions grew in size and influence, the question was raised with increasing frequency whether positive steps, in the form of legislation, were needed to protect the rights of union members (and would-be members) and to ensure that they had as great a voice in the decisions of their union as their union gave them in the decisions of their employer.

One of the first to focus on the question of internal union democracy was the American Civil Liberties Union, whose study "Democracy in Trade Unions," recommending a bill of rights for union members, was published in 1943.[14] During the 1950's there were a number of

[14]Joel Seidman, "Emergence of Concern with Union Government and Administration," in Marten S. Estey, Philip Taft, and Martin Wagner, eds., *Regulating Union Government* (New York: Harper & Row, 1964), p. 4.

governmental investigations into various aspects of union administration, ranging from the 1952–1953 hearings of the New York State Crime Commission on rackcteering along the New York City waterfront (involving the International Longshoremen's Association) to investigations of the mismanagement of union pension funds, which led to the passage of the Welfare and Pension Plans Disclosure Act of 1958.

The last and, by long odds, the most widely publicized of these was the congressional investigation held by the McClellan Committee, or more accurately, the Select Committee on Improper Activities in the Labor or Management Field. From 1957 through 1959 the McClellan Committee held 270 days of hearings, heard 1,526 witnesses, and produced 58 volumes of testimony, over half of which were devoted to evidence of various types of racketeering and corruption in the Teamsters Union. The bulk of the Committee's attention, in fact, was focused on just seven unions out of the more than 180 international unions then active. The risks of generalizing from these limited findings are obvious.[15]

The results of the McClellan Committee hearings were substantial and varied. They made Jimmy Hoffa, then president of the Teamsters, a national figure (albeit a controversial one) and contributed not a little to the public awareness of John F. Kennedy, then a senator, and of his brother Robert. The hearings also led the AFL-CIO to adopt a six-part code of ethical practices and to expel three unions—the Teamsters, the Laundry Workers, and the Bakery and Confectionery Workers—whose leaders were accused of violating these codes. From a public policy standpoint, however, most significant was the impetus they gave for the passage of legislation to correct these abuses—the Labor-Management Reporting and Disclosure Act of 1959, commonly referred to as the Landrum-Griffin Act.

The Landrum-Griffin Act consists of seven sections, or titles; the first six regulate internal union practices, and the seventh contains amendments to the Taft-Hartley Act (as described previously). The first five, which include the basic elements of the law of internal union government, are summarized briefly here.[16]

Bill of Rights

The law begins with a bill of rights for union members, designed to ensure certain standards of democracy within unions and to guarantee the individual due process in his role as a union member. Specifically, the law provides members:

[15]*Ibid.*, pp. 6–7.
[16]*Federal Labor Laws and Programs*, Bulletin No. 262, *op. cit.*, pp. 39–49.

1. Equal right to attend, participate in, and vote at meetings and elections, subject to reasonable union rules.

2. Freedom to meet and assemble with other members, to express any arguments or opinions, and to voice views upon candidates and business properly before a meeting.

3. Protection from increases in dues or the imposition of assessments, except where specified procedures are followed, including secret ballot, referendum, or national union convention.

4. Protection of the right to testify, communicate with legislators, and bring suit for relief (from infringement of rights by the union) after using remedies available to them within the union.

5. The right to copies of bargaining agreements.

6. The right to be informed by the union of their rights under this law.

7. The right to notice and fair hearing before any disciplinary actions are taken against them by the union, except for nonpayment of dues.

When these rights are infringed upon, they are enforced, not by turning to an administrative agency (as in the case of the Wagner and Taft-Hartley Acts), but by filing suit in federal district courts, a procedure which may well tend to reduce the ability of the average union member to use the law for his own protection.

Reporting

Following the bill of rights is the reporting provision, which requires each labor organization to file with the secretary of labor annual financial reports covering its assets and liabilities; a detailed income and expenditures statement, including, among other items, the payments to all union officers, loans to union officers, and loans to businesses; and copies of their constitution and by-laws, with annual reports of any changes made in them. In addition, union officers and employees must report "conflict of interest" financial transactions with businesses the union may deal with; similar reports are required from employers and labor consultants.

The reporting requirement itself is not new; indeed, the Taft-Hartley Act contained a compulsory reporting provision twelve years before the passage of the Landrum-Griffin Act. What is new is that these mandatory union reports became subject to public disclosure. Copies of all reports required by the law are available for inspection or purchase in Labor Department offices; anyone may see them, for any reason.

Public disclosure of financial and administrative details of union government was designed as one of the methods by which the Landrum-Griffin Act would stimulate higher standards of union conduct. As the Bureau of Labor-Management Reports noted in 1960: "The law relies heavily upon the principles of reporting and disclosure to eliminate abuses in the labor-management field. It assumes that democracy in the labor movement is strengthened when union members have detailed essential information about their union and how its affairs are being handled."[17]

Trusteeships

The use of trusteeships—in which national unions take control, for one reason or another, of a local union—is also regulated; the local union is thus protected by the law, just as the individual member is. Basically, the purposes for which trusteeships are permitted are limited, and the national union is required, where a trusteeship continues more than six months, to show why it has not been terminated.

This provision was included in the Landrum-Griffin Act because the McClellan Committee hearings indicated that trusteeships were sometimes used to "milk" local union treasuries or to control local union votes so as to help perpetuate national union officers in power. On the other hand, it was equally clear that trusteeships had a proper function as well and that they were often used to provide assistance to locals in difficulty and to protect the membership from improper conduct of *local* union officers. The problem of devising an effective regulation, therefore, was to distinguish between "proper" and "improper" trusteeships—between "good" and "bad" ones.

In his 1962 report to Congress on the operation of trusteeship provisions, the secretary of labor found 777 trusteeships in effect, covering only 1 percent of all local unions.[18]

Elections

Since elections provide the principal mechanism by which the membership can exercise its role in the government of unions, Congress took steps in the law to ensure both reasonable frequency and regularity of elections and proper election procedures. Accordingly, the law established maximum intervals between union elections of five years for national or international unions, four for intermediate bodies, and three

---

[17]*Report of the Bureau of Labor-Management Reports,* 1960, p. 16.
[18]*Union Trusteeships* (Washington, D.C.: U.S. Department of Labor, Bureau of Labor-Management Reports, 1962), p. 6.

for local unions, and specified standards for the conduct of elections, such as the requirement of secret ballots, provision for a fair chance for the "opposition," and protection of the members' right to vote.

If violations of these election rules appear to have affected the outcome of an election, a court may call for a new election under the supervision of the secretary of labor. While this procedure has been resorted to only infrequently, it was the basis for a dramatic change in the leadership of the United Mine Workers in 1972, when the incumbent, Tony Boyle, was defeated by Arnold Miller in a court-ordered election. The court had set aside Boyle's 1969 re-election because of "massive" violations of the election laws—a charge which had been initiated when Joseph Yablonski, the losing candidate, was murdered shortly after the 1969 election was held. Boyle was subsequently convinced and sentenced to life imprisonment for the Yablonski murder.

Fiduciary Responsibilities

The Landrum-Griffin Act holds that union officers and representatives occupy positions of trust and must, therefore, administer the organization solely for the benefit of its members and in accordance with its own constitutions and by-laws. The act requires officers to be bonded, restricts the uses of union funds, and restricts employer payments and loans to union officials. More important, union officials who are alleged to have violated their trust may be sued, not only by the union, but by the individual union member as well.

Evaluation of Landrum-Griffin Act

The passage of the Landrum-Griffin Act and the experience with its provisions in the twenty-one years since its passage suggest that the key issue lies not in any single provision of the law but in whether it has achieved a better balance than existed before between the rights of individual members on the one hand and the needs of the organization for stability and efficiency on the other. It has become increasingly evident, for example, that greater democracy and a greater rank-and-file voice in union affairs, especially in bargaining and negotiating, is as likely to mean a more militant posture as it is a more flexible one. In many cases, union leaders have found themselves unable to secure ratification of agreements reached with management, and have been forced to return to the bargaining table in search of further concessions.

By 1965, in fact, industrial-relations directors in major industries were publicly admitting their concern over this turn of events and referring wistfully to the days of "responsible" union leadership when a union negotiator could settle on the spot, sure in the knowledge that his membership would accept his recommendations.

Whether this tendency on the whole has become a threat to the effectiveness of collective bargaining and whether it has led to unreasonably expensive economic settlements is not known, and perhaps can never be known. But the issue is no less real because of this; such costs as these must constantly and continually be weighed, however subjectively and inaccurately, against the benefits of greater membership participation in business decision making.[19]

Executive Order 10988

The most significant public policy development in the 1960's was not a law but a presidential executive order, Executive Order 10988, signed by President Kennedy on January 17, 1962. In this order, the president established as a general policy that federal employees had the right to join unions and to bargain collectively, thus extending to them rights provided employees in the private sector by the Wagner Act in 1935. The collective bargaining rights of federal employees, however, are considerably narrower than those of employees in the private sector, for federal employees do not have the right to strike, and their basic economic issues—pay, in particular—are determined in the last analysis, not by collective bargaining, but by the Congress.

E.O. 10988 was replaced in October 1969 by E.O. 11491, which expanded the rights of labor organizations and revised and improved the procedures for handling impasses—unresolved disputes. It did not, however, substantially increase the scope of bargaining.

E.O. 10988 is generally accepted as not only opening the door to unionization of white-collar and professional federal employees, but also providing the impetus for the rapid growth of union membership in state and local government as well. One measure of its impact is that public employees now account for close to 25 percent of the overall membership of labor organizations, having increased from 1.2 million members in 1962, the year E.O. 10988 was issued, to 6 million in 1978.

---

[19]For a recent evaluation of the impact of the act, see Doris B. McLaughlin and Anita L. W. Schoomaker, *The Landrum-Griffin Act and Union Democracy* (Ann Arbor: The University of Michican Press, 1979), pp. vi, 288.

Civil Service Reform Act

The most recent step in bringing federal employees into the mainstream of modern labor relations legislation was the passage of the Civil Service Reform Act of 1978, Title VII of which set forth the law of Federal Service Labor-Management Relations (analogous to the Labor-Management Relations Act of 1947—the Taft-Hartley Act—in the private sector) and established the Federal Labor Relations Authority—the counterpart of the NLRB—to administer it.

The Federal Labor Relations Authority has been in existence only since January 1, 1979, and its full impact remains to be seen. But it is apparent that within the limitations noted above, the legal framework of collective bargaining in the federal service is moving closer to that of the private sector.

The Impact of Collective Bargaining

We have examined the structure and development of labor organizations, how they are managed and how they behave, and the rules of the game under which they operate. Now let us look at the results of their primary activity—collective bargaining—and try to assess its overall impact, both on the employees and managers who are directly affected by the provisions of labor-management agreements and on the general public.

For the sake of discussion, let us examine the impact of labor organizations upon each of these groups in turn—employees, management, and the public.

Impact on Employees

Extent of Direct Impact

Because the law requires that the provisions of collective bargaining agreements must apply to all employees in the bargaining unit, whether they are members of the organization that negotiated the agreement or not, the number of employees covered by collective bargaining agreements exceeds the number who are members of unions and employee associations.

The BLS, in the *Directory of National Unions and Employee Associations, 1977,* estimated that there were approximately 1.8 million nonmembers represented by labor organizations, and that in 1976 approximately 25 million employees in the United States worked under terms of employment determined by collective bargaining.[1]

The Nonwage Impact of Collective Bargaining

These terms of employment are not simply economic issues, for they determine not only how much pay people will get for the work they do but also the rules and regulations of the work place, which largely govern and shape the pattern of life at work—the place where the typical American wage earner spends more of his time than in any other activity except sleeping.

Collective bargaining may be distinguished in several ways from other methods of setting the terms of employment. First, and perhaps most important, is that in contrast to the situation which still prevails in the majority of private business firms and governmental units, where the terms of employment are set unilaterally by management, collective bargaining is a process in which the basic terms of employment are determined *jointly* by the employer and the bargaining representative of the employees; namely, the union or the employee association. Thus, through the collective bargaining activities of their labor organizations, union and association members have a voice in determining the rules which govern their life at work.[2]

Second is the fact that the labor-management agreement establishes contractual rights for employees covered by it, which among other things provide substantial protection against arbitrary discharge or discipline. And, as nonunion plants increasingly match union wages in their efforts to avoid unionization, it may be that one of the chief advantages to workers under collective bargaining will be the contractual rights it gives them—rights which cannot really be duplicated in non-

---

[1]U.S. Department of Labor, Bureau of Labor Statistics, *Directory of National Unions and Employee Associations, 1977,* Bulletin 2044. (Washington, D.C.: U.S. Government Printing Office, 1979), p. 78.

A Current Population Survey made in May 1977 estimated 2.2 million nonmembers covered by collective bargaining agreements, but its estimate of membership was lower than the BLS figures—19.3 million in 1977, as compared to BLS reports of 22.6 million in 1976 and 22.8 million in 1978.

[2]Although the concept that unions "give employees a voice in the government of their industrial life" is not new—see Marten Estey, *The Unions* (New York: Harcourt Brace Jovanovich, 1967), p. 74 and *The Unions,* 2nd ed., 1976, p. 79—significant new insights into that role, including evidence that it can and does have net beneficial effects on the economy, are provided in Richard B. Freeman and James L. Medoff, "The Two Faces of Unionism," *The Public Interest,* Fall 1979, pp. 69–93.

union plants, regardless of how fair or equitable their labor relations may be.

And, finally, the labor-management agreement typically provides a judicial system for enforcing and interpreting the contractual rights of employees, as well as for resolving disputes between employees and managers over the meaning of the agreement—this is the grievance procedure. The grievance procedures in the U.S. collective bargaining system, in fact, are widely considered to be its most distinctive and perhaps its most valuable contribution to industrial relations. Their importance to unions and management is demonstrated in the most recent survey of collective bargaining agreements, which indicate that the grievance procedure was the single most popular provision, being included in 1,508 of the 1,536 agreements analyzed and covering 6.9 million workers, or 98 percent of the survey population. And grievance with arbitration was close behind, covering 6.8 million workers or 97 percent of the survey population.[3]

It should be realized that the grievance procedure is valuable to *both* labor and management, since most agreements with provision for grievance arbitration also include bans on strikes or lockouts during the life of the agreement; the survey just referred to showed 94 percent of all workers subject to such a no-strike clause. To put it another way, the grievance procedure with arbitration as a final step, coupled with a no-strike ban, has resulted in the virtual elimination of strikes as a way to resolve disputes over contract interpretation—a clear benefit to all concerned.

Wages under Collective Bargaining

A key question in considering the impact of unions and collective bargaining is whether or not the wages of employees in unionized firms, which are set by collective bargaining, are generally higher than those in nonunion firms, which management sets unilaterally.[4] Economists refer to this question as one of "relative earnings"—i.e., the earnings of union members relative to those of other workers—or of union-non-union wage differentials.

Although the question of how much impact collective bargaining has on wages is a matter of continuing scholarly debate, and the subject of a voluminous literature, there appears to be general agreement that

---

[3]U.S. Department of Labor, Bureau of Labor Statistics, *Characteristics of Major Collective Bargaining Agreements, January 1, 1978,* Bulletin 2065, April 1980, pp. 105–107.

[4]This is not to be confused with the question whether wages under collective bargaining *rise faster* than nonunion wages and thus contribute more to inflation—that will be discussed separately below.

collective bargaining does make a difference and that union wages average perhaps 15 percent higher than comparable nonunion wages.[5]

Other evidence on this issue comes from the May 1977 Current Population Survey, which found that, "Not surprisingly, workers represented by labor organizations earned more than those that were not. Their usual weekly earnings exceeded those of workers not represented by an average of $41 ($262 compared to $221)."[6] In other words, workers whose wages were determined by collective bargaining earned 18.5 percent more than those not represented by labor organizations.

Interestingly enough, these data also suggest that the economic advantage of union representation is generally greater for blacks and women than for white men. White men covered by collective bargaining agreements earned an average of 6 percent more than those not under collective bargaining, while for women, the advantage was 30 percent, and for blacks it averaged 32 percent (30 percent for men and 34 percent for women).[7]

Union wage differentials may be achieved at the expense of reduced employment in unionized firms; employees laid off by unionized firms (or not hired when the firms fail to expand) may move into the nonunion sector, thus increasing the supply of labor to the nonunion firms (a phenomenon generally referred to as "crowding"), and depressing nonunion wages.

On the other hand, union-nonunion wage differentials may be shrinking due to the "threat effect," the tendency of nonunion firms to match or nearly match union wage rates to reduce the likelihood that their employees will want to unionize, or to ensure their access to qualified labor.

In the public sector, especially among federal employees, where unions generally do *not* bargain over wages (although they do lobby, and intensively so), wages may follow patterns set in the private sector, not because of a threat effect but rather because legislation provides for pay comparability with the private sector.

[5]The classic study of this question is H. Gregg Lewis, *Unionism and Relative Wages in the United States* (Chicago: The University of Chicago Press, 1963). Lewis found that between 1950 and 1958, union wages averaged 14 percent higher than those of nonunion workers.

Most recently, Mitchell has estimated that in the mid-1970s, the differential was probably 20–30 percent. See Daniel J. B. Mitchell, *Unions, Wages, and Inflation,* Washington, D.C.: The Brookings Institution, 1980, pp. 62–112.

[6]U.S. Department of Labor, Bureau of Labor Statistics, *Earnings and Other Characteristics of Organized Workers, May 1977,* Report 556, April 1979, p. 2.

[7]*Ibid.,* Table 10, pp. 28–31. This would be consistent with, and help explain, Kochan's findings that blacks and women are more likely than the general nonunion population to express a preference for joining a union. See Kochan, *op. cit.,* p. 25.

Impact on Management

The most comprehensive study of the impact of collective bargaining on management, Slichter, Healy, and Livernash's monumental 1960 report, suggests that among the most significant effects on management were that:

- Collective bargaining has narrowed the scope of managerial discretion, both by the terms of collective agreements, by the interpretation and administration of those agreements, and by the spread of arbitration as a means of resolving grievances.[8] Indeed, if we view collective bargaining as a means of making (some) management decisions, it is clear that once management recognizes a union as the representative of its employees, it yields its right to make unilateral decisions with regard to many of the terms of employment in favor of sharing those decisions with the union.
- Collective bargaining has "greatly encouraged" the development of management by policy. It is probably fair to conclude that unions have made a major contribution toward rationalizing personnel policies and practices, not only in unionized firms but also in nonunion firms which try to avoid unionization by emulating the practices which prevail in unionized ones. This effect in general would appear to be beneficial to management; Slichter, Healy, and Livernash, in fact, conclude that, "The challenge that unions presented to management has, if viewed broadly, created superior and better-balanced management, even though some exceptions must be recognized," and, "if one single statement were sought to describe the effects of unions on policymaking, it would be 'they have encouraged investigation and reflection.'"[9]

Effects on the Economy and the Public

Efficiency and Productivity

It often seems to a casual observer that whatever benefits collective bargaining has brought the workers have been bought at the price of reduced efficiency and productivity—that seniority, jurisdictional restrictions, and featherbedding, to name a few, interfere with manage-

---

[8]Sumner H. Slichter, James J. Healy, and E. Robert Livernash, *The Impact of Collective Bargaining on Management,* Washington, D.C.: The Brookings Institution, 1960, p. 947.
[9]*Ibid.,* p. 952.

ment's ability to do things in the most efficient manner. The following examples suggest instead that the assessment of the impact of collective bargaining is not that simple, and that it may have positive impacts on efficiency as well.

Among the most frequently cited examples of the adverse effects on efficiency is featherbedding—including the continued employment of workers who as a result of technological change are no longer needed.

But a more sophisticated appraisal suggests that featherbedding is a way of dealing with the human costs of technological change and that the successful adoption of technological change involves a trade-off between increased efficiency on the one hand and the protection of workers' employment needs on the other, with the result that the gains from technological change, rather than being taken exclusively in the form of increased efficiency, are distributed between increased efficiency and productivity on the one hand and the costs associated with cushioning their adverse impacts on employees on the other.[10]

Perhaps nowhere is this more vividly illustrated than in the railroad industry, long identified with the case of the "fireman" on the diesel engine, generally regarded as the epitome of featherbedding. But what is not generally realized is that during the period 1947–1973—the period in which the diesel engine completely supplanted the steam engine in intercity service—labor productivity (or output per man-hour) on Class I railroads rose by an average of 5.2 percent a year, considerably *more* rapidly than the productivity of the economy as a whole, as a direct result of the greater efficiency of the diesel engine. In this case, the so-called featherbedding—the continued employment of firemen— did not prevent the realization of major productivity gains from the new technology; it was a response to the fact that the human cost of this increased productivity was a 66 percent cut in employee man-hours on the railroads, in spite of a slight rise in the volume of business.[11] The featherbedding fireman was trying desperately to avoid a similar fate.

On the other hand, the impact of collective bargaining itself may be to stimulate efficiency. Here the case is often put in terms of the "shock effect"—the argument that union pressure on wages, and hence on costs, forces management into earlier or more frequent searches for labor-saving equipment than would otherwise be the case. To the extent that this is so, unions are in fact hastening the process of technological change, and, thus, whether intentionally or not, providing a constant stimulus to greater efficiency.[12]

[10]See George W. Taylor, *"Collective Bargaining," Automation and Technological Change,* John T. Dunlop, ed., American Assembly, 1962, pp. 84–102.

[11]See U.S. Department of Labor, Bureau of Labor Statistics, *Handbook of Labor Statistics 1975—Reference Edition,* Bulletin 1865, 1975, p. 199.

[12]See Freeman and Medoff, *op. cit.,* pp. 77–82.

Similarly, some industries, such as bituminous coal and trucking, have suffered in the past (and may still) from business overpopulation, with an excessive number of small and inefficient firms struggling to eke out an existence. In such industries, union pressure tends to force out the marginal (inefficient) operators who cannot afford to pay union wages. But whatever this trend does to reduce the prospects of the small businessman in these industries, it seems inescapable that it *raises* the overall efficiency of the industry by weeding out the inefficient.

Are Union Wage Settlements Inflationary?

Because most major collective bargaining agreements are long-term contracts, in which the wage provisions are fixed for three-year periods, wages under such agreements are not responsive to shorter-term changes in economic circumstances (except to the degree provided by escalator clauses)—and, in fact, tend to be what the economists refer to (somewhat disdainfully) as "sticky," both upward and downward. Thus, in an upturn in economic activity, wages under long-term agreements can rise only at rates determined by the contract, which may well be less rapid, or less frequent, than nonunion wages. And, conversely, during slowdowns in economic activity, wage increases already scheduled under collective bargaining agreements will take effect, although in the nonunion sector there may be few if any wage increases.

Furthermore, while severe unemployment among their members may persuade union negotiators to settle for smaller-than-usual *increases,* it is most unlikely that they will accede to wage cuts.

As we have seen, in order to prevent Chrysler's bankruptcy, the Auto Workers were willing to make concessions to it equivalent to $446 million, departing from the GM-Ford pattern mainly by deferring some of its gains. But even though over one-fifth of Chrysler employees were on lay-off at the time of the 1979 negotiations, no wage cuts were made.

In recent years, in fact, it has become evident that while nonunion wages may not increase during a downturn, the resistance to wage *cuts* extends to the nonunion sector as well (again, due in part to the fear that wage cuts would invite unionization). Indeed, as Rees points out, there have been no *general* wage cuts in any major industry since the 1930's—or close to half a century.[13]

And this in turn is due in part to what Okun has called the "invisible handshake"—the implicit contract of employers, whether unionized or

---

[13]Albert Rees, *The Economics of Work and Pay* (New York: Harper and Row, 1973), p. 131.

not, that their employees can expect gradual but continued improvement in their economic position, and, obviously, no wage cuts.[14]

The stickiness of wages under collective bargaining, especially evident during times of recession, raises the question of whether collective bargaining has an inflationary impact.

On this question, as on others we have discussed, ample and authoritative support can be mustered on both sides of the issue. Even such a conservative economist as Milton Friedman has argued that there can be no inflation that is not validated by the Federal Reserve Board; hence, he tends to regard the cost-push approach—the view that it is rising costs, especially labor costs, that push up prices—as invalid.

And, Melvin Reder, in a careful analysis of the problem, concluded that "the responsibility of union wage policy in promoting inflation is greatly exaggerated. . . ."

On the other hand, as Marvin Kosters has pointed out, "Much of the public discussion of inflation is dominated by an emphasis on the behavior of wages [and] . . . the average wage trend has to a large extent been viewed as the central element in the inflation outlook and as the critical variable to which policy should be directed."[15]

But whatever the truth of the matter may be, it is clear that since World War II, seven successive administrations faced with the problem of inflation have acted more or less vigorously on the assumption that the collective bargaining decisions of big unions (and the price decisions of big business) contribute significantly to inflation. And each administration has taken steps, ranging from presidential "jawboning" to statutory control programs, administered by special wage stabilization agencies, to restrain wage increases (especially those under collective bargaining) deemed to be inflationary.[16]

The most recent of these, of course, are those of the Carter administration, which in October 1978 announced a voluntary program for limiting annual increases in wages and fringe benefits to 7 percent annually. In September 1979, following a "national accord" with the leaders of the labor movement, the administration established an eighteen-member Pay Advisory Committee, six members of which represented the labor movement. The guideline was subsequently raised to between 7.5 and 9.5 percent.

---

[14]Arthur Okun, "The Invisible Handshake and the Inflationary Process," *Challenge,* Vol. 22, No. 6, January/February 1980, pp. 6–7.

[15]Marvin Kosters, "Relative Wages and Inflation," *Proceedings, Thirtieth Winter Meeting,* Industrial Relations Research Association, 1977, p. 193.

[16]For a comprehensive analysis of this experience see Crauford D. Goodwin, ed., *Exhortation and Controls: The Search for a Wage-Price Policy 1945–1971* (Washington, D.C.: The Brookings Institution, 1975).

And for the most recent analysis of the wages-inflation issue, see *op. cit.*

For the reader who wishes to judge the evidence for himself, the most recent comparisons of wage changes under collective bargaining with those for the private, nonfarm sector of the economy show that in 1979, effective wage adjustments in major collective bargaining agreements (including current, deferred and COLA adjustments) increased by an average of 9.1 percent, somewhat more than the 7.8 percent increase in average hourly earnings of production and nonsupervisory workers in the private sector. On the other hand, when fringe benefits are taken into account, the first-year adjustments in wages and benefits in contracts covering 5,000 workers or more rose by an average 9 percent as compared with an 8.9 percent gain in total compensation per hour of all employees in the private, nonfarm sector.[17]

And more to the point, the 9 percent first-year increase in collectively bargained wages and benefits and the 8.9 percent gain in hourly compensation in the private sector coincided with an 0.8 percent decrease in productivity (as measured by output per hour of all persons) in the private business sector in 1979. The result was that for the private business sector as a whole, unit labor costs rose in 1979 an average of 10.3 percent—very close to the 11.3 percent increase in consumer prices for the year. One would have to conclude that in 1979, at least, wage behavior in the private business sector as a whole, not just under collective bargaining, contributed to rising prices.

Of course, the big unions fared better than the small ones. In 1979, for example, the five major collective bargaining settlements were in petroleum, trucking, rubber, electrical machinery, and autos. Assuming (unrealistically) an inflation rate of only 8 percent, the annual rates of increase in wages over the life of the contract in these settlements ranged from 7.6 percent in electrical machinery to 10.1 percent in rubber,[18] as compared with an average in all settlements involving 1,000 workers or more of only 6 percent in 1979.

In other words, although public attention focuses on the collective bargaining gains of the Teamsters and the Auto Workers, they are the exception not the rule, so far as union settlements are concerned.

The Impact of Strikes on the Public

One of the ways the general public is affected by the behavior of labor organizations is through the impact of strikes. (It should be emphasized that although strikes are conducted by unions, the responsibility for

[17]See U.S. Department of Labor, Bureau of Labor Statistics, *Major Collective Bargaining Settlements, First Three Months, 1980,* Press Release, April 25, 1980, Table 10, p. 16.
[18]*Economic Report of the President,* 1980, p. 38.

their occurrence is difficult to assess—in any given case, it may fall on either management or the labor organization.)

The impact of strikes has probably been exaggerated by the media. Data on work stoppages in the United States show that for the twenty years 1960–1979, time lost by workers on strike has been consistently less than one-half of 1 percent of total time worked in the economy and has *averaged* less than two-tenths of 1 percent of time worked—the equivalent of only four hours per worker per year.[19] By this measure, the impact of strikes is obviously minimal.

Since these figures do not include time lost by workers affected by, but not involved in, strikes, they somewhat understate total time lost as a result of strikes. But even when we add the numbers of workers laid off or on short hours as a result of a strike elsewhere, the net effect on the economy as a whole tends to be very small.

Thus, the Bureau of Labor Statistics made a special survey of the effect on employment on the strike/lockout in trucking in April 1979. Although it found that between April 8 and 14, 485,000 workers were laid off for at least one day because of interruptions of deliveries, and that aggregate hours were down 3.8 percent in manufacturing and 25 percent in motor vehicle assembly plants, the effect on the economy as a whole was a 1.2 percent reduction in hours in the week of April 8–14—which, as the BLS conceded, "was considerably less than earlier projections."[20]

Regardless of the aggregates, of course, strikes in key industries may have disproportionately severe effects on the public or the economy—indeed, this is the basic assumption underlying the Taft-Hartley national emergency strike provisions.

But the likelihood of national emergency strikes may be less than once anticipated. As we have seen, the resort to the Taft-Hartley emergency strike procedures has declined—it was used only once in the eight-year period 1972–1979, in the bituminous coal strike of 1977–1978, even though, as the Bureau of Labor Statistics pointed out, "the number of all stoppages in the United States reached an all-time high in 1974 ... and seven strikes during 1972–1976 involved 100,000 workers or more each."[21]

Furthermore, the impact on the public of major strikes in durable goods industries tends to be negligible—the General Motors strike of 1970 resulted in 17.8 million man-days lost, and led to a time-lost ratio

[19]Press Release, U.S. Department of Labor, Bureau of Labor Statistics, *Work Stoppages, 1979,* January 1980, p. 3.

[20]"Special Survey Showed 485,000 on Layoff Due to Strike/Lockout in Trucking Industry, April 8–14, 1979," BLS Press Release, April 19, 1979.

[21]U.S. Department of Labor, Bureau of Labor Statistics, *National Emergency Disputes under the Taft-Hartley Act, 1947–77,* Report 542, November 1978, p. 1.

of 0.37 for the year 1970, the highest in the twenty-year period 1960–1979, yet there was no effort to invoke Taft-Hartley, since the consuming public was not seriously affected—they could still buy other makes of new cars as well as used cars.

And strikes involving important services, once regarded as intolerable, have been increasingly treated as inconveniences rather than as threats to the public welfare. The twelve-day 1980 transit strike in New York City was viewed—by the media at least—as more of a challenging event than as a crisis. And even the 1978 coal strike, which took place during an exceptionally severe winter, was considered by the federal judge in the case not to constitute a threat to the public health and welfare sufficient to warrant a Taft-Hartley injunction to bring it to a halt (in fairness, it should be added that the judge also doubted that an injunction would force the miners back to work).

Perhaps the only strikes which are regarded as true threats to public safety are police and firemen's strikes—which are generally illegal. And in many jurisdictions, to avoid illegal strikes, police and firefighters' disputes are subject to compulsory arbitration as a means of dispute resolution.

The reader should also bear in mind that conclusions as to whether strikes have a significant adverse impact on the public or on the economy at large tend to affect one's answer to questions regarding government intervention in strikes. The view that the impact of strikes is exaggerated—a view strongly expressed by George Shultz, secretary of labor under the Nixon administration—supports the conclusion that government intervention in strikes is generally undesirable, if only because it is generally unnecessary.

On the other hand, a belief that strikes jeopardize the national health and safety suggests the need for government to intervene in the public interest. A leading exponent of this view is Arthur Goldberg, secretary of labor in the Kennedy administration.[22] To the extent that these views are perhaps representative of "conservative" and "liberal" political opinion, respectively, it is not without humor that the conservative should regard strikes as insignificant, and the liberal—a former union lawyer—should regard them as a threat to public health and safety!

We conclude that to a significant extent, the impact of strikes on the public is not serious, and that where it would be, alternative dispute settlement mechanisms are available.

Finally, it seems fair to say that strikes are the price that the public must—and is generally willing to—pay if we are to have free collective bargaining rather than regulation of its terms.

[22]*The New York Times,* March 23, 1977.

Epilogue: The Future of Unionism

T he past ninety years have seen the development of two notably successful models of labor organizations—the craft union and the industrial union. Now we are witnessing the evolution of still another form of labor organization—the employee association. Unlike the craft union and the industrial union, the employee association did not originate as a labor organization designed for collective bargaining, but typically as a professional society or as a state civil service employees' lobby. Only lately has it taken on the responsibilities of employee representation and collective bargaining that lead us to regard it as a labor organization.

A question remains, however, whether the employee association will attract significant numbers of members that cannot be reached by labor unions, or whether it will simply become interchangeable with them, competing with them for the same employees. At present, employee associations consist very largely of state and local government employees, the majority of whom are school teachers; less than 10 percent of their total membership is found in the private and nonprofit sectors. And although they are the dominant model of labor organization in both education and in state and local government, employee associations have certainly not supplanted unions in either case. In fact, the State, County and Municipal Employees, which competes with the state public employee associations, and the American Federation of Teachers, which competes with the National Education Association, ranked first and second among major unions in terms of growth rates between 1968 and 1978. It is generally accepted that competition from unions was instrumental in forcing the employee associations to adopt union behavior and to assume the collective bargaining function.

143

As was the case in the 1930's, when competition between craft and industrial unions contributed to the growth of union membership, competition between associations and unions for the right to represent teachers and state and local government employees has been beneficial to the labor movement as a whole, contributing to the upsurge in membership of public employees and white-collar workers, as well as demonstrating that both employee associations and unions can meet the needs of such employees.

But so far, employee associations have done relatively little to bring collective bargaining to professional employees in the private and nonprofit sectors. Only 166,000 members, or less than 7 percent of the total employee association membership, are employed outside the public sector.

The recent activities of professional employees in private, nonprofit institutions such as hospitals and private colleges and universities suggest that they may prefer professional associations to unions, and that they are ready to turn to collective bargaining.

But the history of organization between 1968 and 1978 indicates that once professional employees turn to collective bargaining as a way of determining their conditions of employment, the key question becomes that of choosing the most effective bargaining representative, and the door is opened to union competition within the employee association.

In the competition for membership of professional employees, the question is which organizational model will win—the union or the employee association, or perhaps some hybrid version of the two?

Index